Bertolucci's *1900*

BERTOLUCCI'S
1900

A NARRATIVE AND HISTORICAL ANALYSIS

Robert Burgoyne

Wayne State University Press
Detroit

Copyright © 1991 by Wayne State University Press,
Detroit, Michigan 48202. All rights are reserved.
No part of this book may be reproduced without formal permission.
95 94 93 92 91   5 4 3 2 1

Library of Congress Cataloging-in-Publication Data

Burgoyne, Robert, 1949–
    Bertolucci's 1900 : a narrative and historical analysis / Robert Burgoyne.
        p.   cm. — (Contemporary film and television series)
    Includes bibliographical references.
    ISBN 0–8143–2083–X (alk. paper)
    1. 1900 (Motion picture)   I. Title.   II. Series.
PN1997.A2133B87 1991
791.43′72 – dc20   90–12355
                                                                                 CIP

For Tova and Brian

CONTENTS

Contents

PREFACE

A Note on the Two Versions of *1900*

There are two versions of *1900* in current release: each can be considered complete and authentic. The five-hour and twenty-minute European release and the four-hour American version are entirely the products of Bertolucci's hand. The four-hour American version was edited by the director approximately one year after completion of the European version, after many disputes with the American producer and distributor, Paramount.

In choosing the American version for my analysis, I was guided by Bertolucci's own assessment of this version as the stronger of the two. In an interview with Deborah Young (1977), Bertolucci made the following comments:

> It's very difficult to say what's been cut because almost no sequence was entirely cut out. I tried to cut in a way not to impoverish the film . . . Although the structure remains the same, almost all the sequences are still in the film, what's been changed is the rhythm, and this alters a film very much. It's all more tachycardic, like a fast heartbeat. Before it was bradycardic, the opposite. Now it's anxious. But I think that perhaps I like the film better now than before.
>
> *They didn't suggest any cuts to you?*
>
> No, no, I was completely free . . . once I discovered they weren't trying to castrate me, but that there was a chance of bettering the film, I became excited about the work, I saw things from a new angle.

One additional reason recommends the American version: the fact that the principal actors speak in their own voices. In the European release, the voices of Burt Lancaster, Sterling Hayden, Robert De Niro, etc.,

1

are all dubbed into Italian by Italian actors. The absence of vocal authenticity in the case of an actor such as Burt Lancaster is disconcerting in the extreme. It has the effect of seeming to alter the actor's appearance, and it definitely transforms the actor's and the character's personality. The acting in the film is enriched by the retention of the actors' natural voices. Although this aspect of the text is not a part of my analysis, it has certainly played a part in shaping my response to the film. For this reason, and because Bertolucci himself seems to regard the American version as the more "finished" film, I have based my analysis on the more recent of the two releases.

A close scrutiny of the two versions indicates that Bertolucci's assessment of the changes is entirely accurate. Nothing that can be considered substantive has been eliminated. The first difference is found directly after the birth of Alfredo. The American version deletes the scene in which the elder Alfredo Berlinghieri enters the wine cellar on the estate, drawing bottles from the racks to celebrate and the comic dialogue between Rigoletto, the peasant jester, the Padrone, and the local priest that follows. The next scene, in which the characters enter the fields to toast the births of Alfredo and Olmo, is identical in both releases. Other events that are cut from the American release also have something of a comic quality to them. Just prior to his suicide, for example, the elder Alfredo is shown in the European version listening to a peasant waltz, complaining that he doesn't even have enough breath to give an order to a servant anymore, and giving a kiss to a pig. Both the European and American releases then show the Padrone soliciting the little peasant girl, Emma.

The one episode that is entirely cut from the American version is a scene at night wherein the peasants are discussing the upcoming strike. The elder Dalco, Leo, warns the men of what they will become after months of no work and no food. The younger men respond by saying that individually, yes, they are weak, but the "League" is strong. They raise a slogan that is picked up by workers throughout the fields, making the landscape resound with shouts of solidarity. The elder Dalco at this points says, "I like this song" and picks up the slogan himself.

Other changes are extremely minor. After Attila's introduction at the farm, for example, in which he asserts the philosophy of the landowners, Anita, later to be Olmo's wife, calls on the peasant women to resist and begins showering Attila with grain. All the peasant women join in. In the American version, the scene ends with Anita exhorting the peasant women, while the camera simply lingers on Attila's somewhat surprised face. Other scenes are curtailed in this fashion as well. The sex scene between Alfredo and Ada in the hay is shorter and considerably less graphic in the Amer-

2

ican release. The scene wherein the two snort cocaine with Alfredo's uncle Ottavio appears without the European version's fairly lengthy treatment of how Ottavio obtained the cocaine. And the American release minimizes the brutal confrontation between Ada and Regina after Ada has descended into drunkenness during her long twilight period in the villa. In the longer version, Ada pours a bottle of wine over Regina's head, saying, "I baptize you pig woman!" Finally, at the end of the American film, the utopian celebration of the peasants is played without a group of characters who have just arrived "from the mountains," and who must be educated, on the spot, in the values of communism.

The American version, in most cases, has eliminated only inessential material, material that tends to diffuse the central message of the film. In one scene — the preparation for the confrontation on the road between the strikers and the cavalry — the editing clarifies the symbolic geometry of the sequence and highlights the conflictual dynamic of the opposing classes. The European release is far less effective and even somewhat confusing in its visual treatment of this scene. For example, the European version begins the scene with a circular scan of the landscape, roughly from the peasants' point of view. We then get a series of close-ups of worried-looking peasants. The film then cuts to Alfredo and Regina in the distant part of the fields, showing Alfredo masturbating Regina with his rifle, and Regina expressing definite dissatisfaction. Next, we get a shot of the landowners gliding in their boats on the water, hunting ducks. Finally, the cavalry is seen, massing on the road. It is very difficult to synthesize all these seemingly disparate elements.

This difficulty is resolved in the American release, in what is one of the most dramatic and well-crafted scenes in the film. The revised version begins with a shot of the cavalry on the road, providing us with an immediate image of menace and threat. Gunfire is heard, startling the horses. We then cut to several close-ups of ducks falling into the water, followed by a shot of several small boats with the hunters standing in them moving slowly along the waterway. The initial connection between the landowners and the soldiers is thus established acoustically by the gunshots. Rather than beginning the sequence with the peasants before we have the knowledge of the imminent threat that faces them, the American release first establishes the menace in the form of the cavalry, the agency behind the menace in the figures of the landowners, and the possible outcome in the shots of dying waterfowl.

Only then are the peasants introduced; their successful resistance begins here with a long shot of workers in heavy-laden carts moving into the foreground of the frame. A moving camera shot gives us close-up portraits of Anita and of the other peasant women. At this point, a distant shout is heard; the peasants begin calling to one another to abandon their carts and resist. The camera commences a 360° pan that encompasses the entire landscape, bringing into view the line of peasants and, at the end of its scan, the line of cavalry. The remainder of the scene unfolds identically in both versions.

The editing of the revised version not only clarifies the actual content of the scene, but provides a clear linkage between the landowners and the soldiers, both of whom are associated with domination through force: both nature and the peasants are shown as subject to the depredations of the landowners and their surrogates, the soldiers. In the case of the peasants, the geometry of space and the call and response vocal gestures link the peasants to the landscape and to the larger domain of nature. The circular pan now serves as the centerpiece of this portion of the scene, providing a kind of visual symbolism that can be contrasted to the montage of dying waterfowl and gunshots that constituted the focal point of the segment detailing the landowners and the cavalry.

The other significant change that Bertolucci conceived for the American release concerns the scene at the very end of the film involving Olmo and Alfredo as two old men, shoving and wrestling each other to the train tracks where they undertook their test of courage during their youthful years. In the European release, the film depicts the final moments of the two principals without juxtaposing different moments in time. They remain old men throughout the scene, with the exception of one brief "memory" of their younger days that seems to flash up momentarily. In the American release, by contrast, the filmmaker intercuts several shots of the old men as boys and dwells on the youthful version of the two protagonists. As the film ends, the final shot consists of the young Alfredo lying beneath the train, as if time has been refashioned in a circular form and had looped back to start the process over again. As I argue in Chapter seven, the section on symbolic patterning in *1900*, this is a significant scene in the film, the culmination of a pattern of renewal and regeneration that serves to countermand the linear model of time and historical process that conventionally structures the historical text.

I have found, in short, that the American version has gained something from Bertolucci's revisions. The loss of content through the trimming of scenes can safely be described as minute. But the advantages realized through the editing of certain scenes are substantial. Coupled with the retention of the actors' natural voices, the American version can in fact be seen not as a diminished version, an attenuated "translation," but rather as the stronger of the two renditions.

ACKNOWLEDGMENTS

I would like to thank Annette Michelson for her gracious assistance in helping me embark on this project, and for the many ways in which she has been my advocate over the years. I would also like to thank Bill Simon, whose timely support, generosity, and commitment to the success of this work were vital to its completion. My special appreciation goes to David Nelson and his devoted staff at the Wayne State University Word Processing Center. Thanks also to the College of Liberal Arts of Wayne State University for helping defray the costs of photographic reproduction. The stills are reproduced from the Museum of Modern Art; Courtesy of Paramount Pictures. To Lee Schreiner, whose faith in this book brought it into being, I offer my heartfelt thanks. To Robin DuBlanc, who edited this book with sympathy and exactitude, I give my appreciation. Finally, I would like to express my deep gratitude to Tom Conley, whose swift and inspired comments guided my writing, and whose passion for critical analysis set me on the path of film study.

A slightly different version of chapter four, "Temporality as Historical Argument in *1900*" was published in *Cinema Journal* 28. 3 (Spring 1989): 57–68. A slightly different version of chapter seven was published as "The Somatization of History in Bertolucci's *1900*" in *Film Quarterly* 40. 1 (Fall 1986): 7–14.

INTRODUCTION

This study concerns itself, most broadly, with the narrative structuration of history in Bernardo Bertolucci's *1900*. I argue that the fictional techniques employed in the film — its concentration on dual protagonists who begin as friends and wind up as opponents, its well-defined patterns of conflict and resolution, its overall orientation to a culminating end point — should be understood not as distortions of an "authentic" order of events, but as highly refined modes of historical argument, analogous to established techniques such as explanation by epitome, the linking of cause and effect, and the refiguring of temporal process into a significant pattern. Moreover, the text articulates an overall theory of history through its narrative patterning — particularly in its control of the temporal dimension — that gives unity and scope to the different symbolic resolutions that emerge at the levels of plot, character roles, and focalization. By clarifying the points of contact between fictional and historical forms of representation, this study establishes an enriched context not only for the analysis of *1900* but also for the examination of the genre of the historical film.

Although the restaging of the historical past has emerged as one of the central forms of cultural expression in the present day, the historical film is generally free of the irony and ambivalence that characterize the use of historical styles in painting and architecture, for example. While an interest in historical elements animates many contemporary art forms, the genre of the historical film has achieved a special kind of cultural legitimacy and importance. The ascendance of the historical film — most patently visible, in this country, in the proliferation of works dealing with Vietnam — suggests that film has received a kind of sanction, a mandate to represent the past, as if it is through the film medium that the codes and motifs expressing the collective imaginary relation to history can best be articulated. Long considered to be little more than a "costume" genre, the historical film is now valued as a significant document that illuminates not only the period it reenacts, but also the period in which it was made.

The critical study of the historical film, however, has been hindered by an inadequate methodology. Until very recently, critical analysis was limited to discussions of a film's accuracy: its fidelity to a supposedly factual order of events or its faithfulness in characterization. The film was explicitly compared to the existing state of historical knowledge, with the standard of authenticity prevailing over the variables of interpretation. Lately, however, the historical film has been the recipient of a much more sophisticated scrutiny. Studies by Pierre Sorlin, Marie-Claire Ropars, Marc Ferro, Natalie Zemon-Davis, and others have treated the genre from a variety of perspectives, all of which are informed by current thinking in critical theory. Structuralism, semiotics, psychoanalysis, deconstruction, and an approach that might be called, after Umberto Eco, the "logic of culture," now structure critical discourse on the historical film in terms not of realism or resemblance to a known referent, but in terms of its underlying logic. However, with the exception of the occasional and useful analysis by Sorlin, the discourse of narrative theory—the model most attuned to the analysis of traditional historical techniques of explanation and argument and most geared to the central questions of authority, temporality, and the weighing of competing perspectives—has not yet been employed.

In part because narrative theory has only recently been extended to film, and in part because of the suspicion with which narrative historical writing has been regarded, the narratological analysis of the historical film would seem to be afflicted with a double set of handicaps. Firstly, there are several characteristics intrinsic to the film medium that make narrative analysis somewhat difficult to apply. One of the most daunting problems centers on the cinematic narrator, understood as the illocutionary source or instance of emission of the narrative discourse. Because film is a visual rather than a verbal medium and does not imply a literal speaker or hearer, some theorists argue that the need to designate a narratorial source for the representation of the fictional world is obviated: the events of the fictional world simply "tell themselves," in the words of Emile Benveniste. Other theorists maintain that because film communicates messages to a viewer, filmic discourse involves a sender (or addresser), and a receiver (or addressee) in a communicative situation. These two different positions on the cinematic narrator are not merely a matter of theoretical debate: they have distinct pragmatic and interpretive consequences as well. The issue of the cinematic narrator is especially significant in the reading of films that involve narratorial commentary, evaluation, or argumentation, such as the historical film. In the chapters that follow, I will argue for a theory of the cinematic narrator based primarily on the control and manipulation of the system of tense in film.

Secondly, narrative analysis would appear to reinforce the "fictional" aspect of the historical film, definitively displacing the focus of interest from the representation of actual historical forces and occurrences to that of imaginary events, thus subtracting from the historical film its most salient characteristic: the focus on the historical past. It is in fact the case that narrative analysis does not distinguish between actual and fictional occurrences appearing in a narrative form. If these occurrences are emplotted, ascribed to an agent, described from a certain angle of perception, and equipped with evaluative or judgmental commentary, it matters not, as far as narrative analysis is concerned, whether these events actually occurred or whether they were invented. This, of course, is not only true of narrative analysis, but of many contemporary theories of discourse, to the extent that the formerly absolute distinction between realistic and imaginative discourses based on the different status of their referents has been replaced by the recognition that semiological processes systematically substitute signifeds for referents, mental concepts for the "real" ostensibly delivered by realistic or historical writing. As Hayden White emphasizes, the difference between realistic and fictional discourses based on the ontological difference between their referents, real and imaginary, is dissolved in semiological theory; instead, there is a concentration on systems of producing discursive meaning, of which narrative is a particularly effective and universal mode.

In contemporary historiography, narrative form has been substantially rehabilitated, with major studies by Paul Ricoeur, Hayden White, and Paul Veyne stressing the unique power of narrative structure in rendering historical events. The political value of narrative representation has also been reconsidered. Once identified as the vehicle of bourgeois ideology in its most transparent manifestation — with the features of closure, individual agency, and linear "progress" defining both the form and its content — recent Marxian theory has discovered that narrative is well-suited to convey the "social movement by which a unity of meaning can be imposed upon the chaos of history" [White 1987, 157]. Far from simply reproducing the dominant power relations of the bourgeois world, the "prestidigitation of narrative" makes it possible to imagine a creative alternative to the "real conditions of existence." This is well expressed by White in a review of the work of Fredric Jameson: "Narrativity not only represents, but justifies, by virtue of its universality, a dream of how ideal community might be achieved" (1987, 157).

With the advances made on these two fronts—the extension of narrative theory to film and the redemption of narrative form as a legitimate method in historical and political theory—a searching analysis and critique of the historical film can now be developed. In this study, I will focus on narrative analysis as a means of disclosing a range of historical arguments and interpretations in *1900*. The film focuses on two protagonists, one a peasant, the other a member of the bourgeoisie, who are born on the same estate on the same day in 1901. As the century unfolds, the two friends become increasingly antagonistic and hardened in their class positions. Peasant strikes, World War I, the rise of the Fascist party, and the worsening persecution of the peasantry lead finally to the culminating Day of Liberation, April 21, 1945, when a kind of peasant utopia is briefly realized. On this day, the peasants are in the ascendant, and the Padrone, representative of the old bourgeoisie, appears, for a moment, to be historically obsolete. The film then cuts ahead to the future, to show the two protagonists, now old men, still wrestling and disputing with each other.

In the detailed analysis that follows, I argue that the narrative form of the film expresses a sophisticated, highly refined historical analysis in which the past is interpreted, in a Marxian fashion, as a prefiguration of a new society to be achieved in the present and the future. These arguments are woven into the narrative language of the film, and are in fact expressible, I maintain, only in the symbolic language of narrative. The historical argument fashioned through the temporal patterning of the film, for example, can be articulated only indirectly, through the type of symbolic trajectory that narrative alone affords.

There are three principal reasons for privileging narrative analysis, as opposed to other methods, for the study of *1900*. Firstly, narrative form, in its more sophisticated manifestations, involves a variety of laminated perspectives and competing voices that provide a very dense modeling of events and the network in which they occur. This muliplicity, this layering of perspectives, approximates in *1900* the complexity of historical processes and places in the foreground the competing agendas at work in the representation of the historical past. Each stratum of the work emits its own message; each in turn is linked hierarchically to the other layers. Narrative analysis is uniquely suited to register the diverse voices and multiple perspectives that characterize a work such as *1900*.

Secondly, the "content of the form," to borrow a phrase from White, is articulated chiefly through the film's narrative structure. Specifically, the film's political message, and especially its recovery of the visionary

10

or utopian theme in Marxism — a theme that has been repressed or forgotten in many Marxian analyses — emerges through the simultaneous articulation of the actual history of class struggle and the possible history of a utopian future embedded within it. Moments of struggle are recoded in such a way that local, historical events acquire a secondary referent. This double-coding can be understood as a kind of shift in perspective, manifested through the temporal and point of view structures of the film. I argue that this shift in perspective can be taken as a causal force in history, "opening out a prospect that makes . . . a new kind of action possible in one's future," thus affecting the historical past itself (White, 1987, 150). The notion of a shift in perspective as a causal force in history is made especially clear, White argues, in the case of revolutionary societies, who may elect to rewrite all or part of their past history in order to bring into relief events formerly regarded as unimportant. In *1900*, what emerges is a kind of "anamorphic" history — the chronicled historical event and the recoding of that event from the perspective of the peasantry, as if it were perceived from the vantage of the future.

Thirdly, only in narrative form can the elusive and fundamental experience of temporality be expressed. According to Ricoeur, historical writing and fictional writing share a common "ultimate referent": the structures of temporality. Through the device of emplotment, historical writing effects a mediation between a mere sequence of events and the universal human experience of temporality, which lends the events significance and scope. Moreover, the structures of temporality convey the political message of the film in the most far-reaching fashion. Here, the theory of history animating the film comes into prominence, as the temporal structures of the work articulate the "genealogical" project of the work: the past conceived not as an immutable, determinate order that inescapably imprints the present, but rather the past apprehended as open and responsive to the present and the future.

The central proposition that informs the narrative approach to the historical film is that the argument or philosophy of history that is set forth in *1900*, or, for that matter, in the historical film generally, takes shape not in details of costume or period setting, but primarily through narrative patterning — the conversion of a sequence of events into a web of cause and effect relationships, the linking of part to whole, the foregrounding of the impact and the limitations of human agency and, above all, the conversion of historical time into narrative temporality. Through narrative patterning, the historical film is vested with the power of historical explanation. Moreover, through narrative patterning one of the chief requirements of contemporary historical analysis can be articulated: the foregrounding of alternate modes of analysis, the methodological acknowledgement that there are different ways of telling the story, and that different interpretive possibilities exist.

Natalie Zemon-Davis (1988) stresses this quality — the indication of different versions or the possibility of multiple tellings — as characteristic of contemporary historiography. Certain films, such as Carl Dreyer's *Day of Wrath*, she claims, possess a structure analogous to this attribute of historical writing: the events in *Day of Wrath*, as in the genre of the fantastic as analyzed by Tzvetan Todorov, can be interpreted both as natural and as supernatural; either explanation is possible at any point in the narrative. In Bertolucci's *1900*, a similar superimposition of perspectives occurs. Different interpretive possibilities exist at every point, as the film superimposes what might be called comic and tragic versions of the historical process. In fact, very different generic messages are emitted by the film.

Even more tellingly, the work of narrative analysis, in dividing the text into different strata, reveals very different problems and solutions of historical interpretation at each separate level of the text. Thus the plot structure focuses on one set of concerns and offers a formal pattern that seems to indicate a type of resolution. Specifically, the events of the plot, taken in isolation, appear to stress the power of the bourgeoisie, who seem to command all of the active Moves; the peasants appear to be the "Patients" of history, rather than the "Agents." But this level of the text is precisely contradicted by another aspect of the narrative design, namely, the system of tense. The temporal dimension of the film recodes the bare, punctual events of the plot in such a way that the seeming victims of historical forces can be perceived as the ultimate victors, stressing the accelerated decline of one class and the ascendancy of another. A similar disparity can be discerned in the dynamic relation between what might be called narrative voice and narrative point of view, or focalization. While the narratorial "slant" appears to endorse the peasant enterprise, in ways I will designate, the focalization resides for the most part with the bourgeoisie and the Fascists, who provide the principal "angle of view" on events. The film, moreover, emits very different generic messages in its structuring of the character-system. While the character of Olmo, the peasant leader, is rendered in an epic, idealized fashion, the character of Alfredo, the bourgeois Padrone, is portrayed in a highly psychologized manner, with the nuances of his sexuality, his neuroses, and his ambivalence toward the peasants frankly displayed. These competing perspectives and discordant generic signals deliver messages in their own right and cue us to the diversity of forms assembled in the text, a diversity that brings into view the complexity, the multiplicity, of history itself.

12

Although the form of the film illustrates in an especially clear way the sense in which emplotment can be conceived as historical argument and interpretation, there may still be reservations about narrative form in general, which for many readers might appear to issue an overall message that could be perceived as at odds with the Marxian political argument energizing the text. The film builds a historical argument through the device of epitome — the historical conflict of the two classes is embodied, epitomized, in the story of the two characters. *1900*'s epic structure — an opening *in medias res*, the encapsulation of the rise and fall of two classes through the deeds of two protagonists, its teleological orientation, where the end can be found in the beginning and the entire structure is immanent in each of the parts — conforms to established principles of narrative construction. It is precisely this type of narrative patterning of history that Louis Althusser so thoroughly critiques. The famous dictum: "History is a process without a telos or a subject" (Althusser 1984) can be taken as a repudiation of just this form of generic overlap between fictional narrative and the writing of history, where the agents or history become assimilated to the agents of narrative, and where the orientation to the future imposes a predetermined form on historical events.

The most glaring example of the "historicism" that Althusser objects to is the Marxian "master narrative" of history, with its succession of historical stages or sequences of modes of production, from the primal hoard to the clan, from the feudal system to capitalism, with the end point projected as the inevitable final stage of world Communism. Marxian historicism, a "providential history," is organized, like a perspective drawing, around a temporal vanishing point, a limit point at the end of history, to which all the occurrences of the world lead. Althusser, on the other hand, conceives of history as an "absent cause," identifying it with Lacan's Real as "that which resists symbolization absolutely." Thus history, seen as the unmediatable, unapproachable Real, cannot be "reflected" in discursive form, cannot be expressed or represented; it can be known only as a kind of postulate, nowhere present, but everywhere "effective."

In many ways, this critique strikes at the heart of Bertolucci's project in *1900*. The succession of modes of production depicted in the film, its orientation to a utopian end point, its concentration on individual protagonists, and its express sense of the competence of its narrative form to convey the human truth of history, place it in stark opposition to a more "scientific" approach such as would be favored by Althusser. But there are other Marxian critics who offer defenses of narrative form precisely for the message it sends forth concerning history and society. The narrative form in which history is cast bears witness to a positive impulse, an impulse to mediate and fold together "reality" (the actual occurrences) and imagination (the scenario of a possible or potential order of real events). In the view of Fredric Jameson, this productive mediation is best exemplified by that self-same Marxian "master narrative" of history, which projects a vision of human liberation and redemption as the final stage of social process, a utopian transformation of all human society, a dimension that all the local conflicts and discord of the world anticipate (Jameson 1981). For Jameson, the fact that history can be apprehended primarily through narrative form is a cause for optimism, for it signals a concealed utopianism, a collective imaginary yearning, whose articulation is one of the intrinsic features of narrative: "in its purely formal properties, the dialectical movement by which a unity of plot is superimposed upon the superficial chaos of story-elements, narrative serves as a paradigm of the kind of social movement by which a unity of meaning can be imposed upon the chaos of history" (White 1987, 157). The power of narrative to reveal in a sequence of historical events a prefiguration of a project to be accomplished in the future makes it possible to imagine a creative alternative to the "real conditions of existence."

Jameson acknowledges Althusser's general point concerning the absent and inaccessible nature of the historical "fact," history itself, but supplies a missing piece of the argument: history, as an absent cause, is inaccessible as such; it can be approached, therefore, only in textual form, only through its prior textualization, its narrativization in the political unconscious (Jameson 1981, 53). This point is reinforced throughout *The Political Unconscious*: "history is not a text, not a narrative, master or otherwise . . . although it is inaccessible to us except in textual [or narrative] form" (1981, 82). Although the rendering of history seemingly cannot escape determination by textual and narrative form—complete with a *telos* and a subject—this very cloaking lends the "story" a universal significance, freeing it from its time-bound and narrow focus. The Marxian narrative of history constitutes a case in point: it is the "amplitude" of its pattern, the "narrativity of that structure," that gives it its imaginative power, its ability to unite "all of the individual stories of societies, groups and cultures into a single great story" (White 1987, 148).

1900 articulates these themes in a direct fashion, employing a narrative structure that is specifically designed to "restore the traces of that uninterrupted narrative" (Jameson 1981, 20) to the manifest level of the text. The film expresses through its narrative patterning the sense of the continuity of societies as well as the dissolution of certain classes and folds together actual and possible events in a way that calls forth the historical imagination and permits a kind of visionary history to emerge. Bertolucci's own

14

comments on this aspect of the film are instructive. Concerning the framing event that orients the dramatic structure of *1900*, he says: "It's a day, the 25th of April, 1945, the Italian Day of Liberation, and it includes the whole century. We took it as a sort of symbolic day on which is unleashed, on which flowers this peasants' utopia . . . This day of utopia contains the century. It's a temporal unit, a very special day, different from all the others. The premise of this day lies in the past, but the day also contains the future." And: "there is always an intervention on the level of fantasy in order to arrive at the fundamental points of the historical process of the formation of political consciousness" (Bertolucci 1975, 12, 16).

Finally, the film's highly patterned temporal structure communicates a set of messages that, I believe, can only be expressed in the symbolic language of narrative. Paul Ricoeur, in a two-volume study of the shared narrative features of historical and fictional writing entitled *Time and Narrative*, has stressed the conclusive similarity of narrative fiction and historical writing in their common "ultimate referent" — the structures of temporality. Both historical writing and fiction illuminate and give symbolic form to the most elusive yet penetrating structure of human experience, the experience of time. This ultimate referent or content is embodied in narrative form itself, for narrative "is the language structure that has temporality as its ultimate referent" (Ricoeur 1980, 169).

In contrast to the older narrativist tradition of historical writing, in which real historical events seemed to fit the pattern and display the forms of traditional story-types — history as a species of "lived stories" waiting to be commited to prose — Ricoeur argues that historical events possess the same structure as narrative discourse primarily because of their mutual involvement with the structures of temporality. This emerges through "emplotment," which mediates between the actual events, on the one hand, and the human experience of time that lends to these events the "aura of historicality" on the other. Narrative fiction may deal with imaginary events and history with real events, but these are only their immediate referents; these events become meaningful only when they are emplotted in a fashion that opens up to the fateful processes of time. History and literature resemble each other because both are speaking about the same thing — the structures of temporality, which can only be addressed in the symbolic language of narrative.

It is in this sense that I conceive the configuring not only of time, but also of imaginary and historical events in *1900*. Rather than distinguishing the fictive from the actual historical incidents in the film, I analyze the form of emplotment, the narrative structure, which lends them both a single, ultimate referent. The term emplotment covers several different strata of the text: the syntax of events, the "spheres of action" or, better, the "narrative domains" of the various characters, the control of point of view and the patterning of narrative temporality, as well as other aspects of narrative form. Although each level of the text produces a distinct message concerning the historical and political conflicts the film depicts — and here the dynamic character of emplotment is foregrounded — there is in each case an appeal to a "secondary referent," an overarching thesis that unifies the text around a symbolic center: a concept of time that exceeds the determinism of past, present, and future. This focus on temporality ultimately expresses the political message of the film; it is here that the overall theory of history informing the film can be discerned. The historical past is seen not as a closed, sealed world, not as an immutable order of events, but rather as episodes in an "unfinished plot" whose meaning is not fixed; the past apprehended as containing the "conditions of possibility" leading to the film's utopian resolution. Rather than seeing the past as an immobile form, safely to the rear of the present, the film views the past as riding on a parallel track alongside the present, constantly pressuring it; in turn, the present reshapes and remolds the past for its own ends.

The historical film in general utilizes techniques that are identical with traditional forms of historiographic analysis: *1900* employs these analytic categories, such as cause and effect analysis and explanation by epitome, and renders these techniques for the most part through its control of the temporal dimension. It goes beyond traditional historiography, however, to essay an approach to the historical past that can be described as genealogical or "narratological": a "willing backward" to focus on the past not as an established, known, and conclusive order that has evolved ineluctably into the present, but as a particular set of possibilities that can be realized in the future. As White explains: "human beings can will backward as well as forward in time; willing backward occurs when we rearrange accounts of events in the past that have been emplotted in a given way, in order to endow them with a different meaning or to draw from the new emplotment reasons for acting differently in the future" (1987, 150).

By attending closely to the overall narrative patterning of the film, the explanatory value of narrative form can be discerned. The form makes intelligible elusive relationships that cannot be broached except in symbolic language, a factor that recommends narratological analysis for its ability to bring to light structures that are indistinct in the densely layered composition of the narrative artifact. Moreover, the fundamental ques-

16

tion of what accounts for the compelling interest of a historical work can be addressed. As Ricoeur writes: "It is this interest that assures the continuity between history based on historiography and ordinary narration" (1984, 151). What is perhaps most challenging, is that in this work we can begin to apprehend the role of emplotment even when history has ceased to be a history of events, strictly speaking, and has instead become a history of emergent or nascent forces that prefigure a new social order.

Unlike others who have treated the problem, I will not separate the historical and the fictional sequences into separate genres, such as the spectacle versus the romance, for the animating principles of *1900* are to be found in both registers, and in fact depend on the commingling of the two: the genealogical project of the film consists precisely in the willing backward to "rearrange accounts of events in the past that have been emplotted in a given way" (White 1987, 150). The intermingling of fictional or imaginative events and actual occurrences is a crucial factor in this willing backward, and it is through the combination of fictional passages and historical framework that the large-scale historical enterprise of the film takes shape.

Following a prefatory chapter dealing with the relation between narrative structure and the modeling of history, a topic that has been the subject of several recent books, I will present a detailed narratological analysis of *1900*. The chief task of this analysis is the precise breakdown and description of the narrative strategies and techniques used to render historical events. The actual analysis of *1900* is not dependent on the chapter on historiography, and the reader may confidently skip ahead to the analysis of the film, if he or she desires. Each level of the narratological analysis of the film will be preceded by a short summary of the theoretical literature on this particular narratological topic. The actual narrative analysis of *1900* will consist of three levels — the functional, or syntactic level of plot events, which I have called, after Thomas Pavel, the *Move* structure; the analysis of the *dramatis personae*, in which I shall discuss the various characters and the separate "narrative domains" they inhabit; and the study of the narrational level, stressing the categories of Tense, Mood, and Voice, in which the relations of temporality, point of view, and narrative "voice" are discussed. As examples of narrative voice, I shall discuss such textual properties as editing and camera movement, relating these formal properties to the deep-structural forms of historical argument disclosed above. Finally, I will conclude with a reading of the film's symbolic structure.

In treating the film in this layered manner, it will become clear that different problems of historical interpretation surface at different levels of the text. But the basic difficulty the work confronts can be stated quite simply: the film must disclose a homology between the fate of the individual subject and the fate of an entire people. The different problems and solutions posed at different levels of the film revolve around this central concern; in offering a range of perspectives, the film underscores the complexity of historical interpretation. In the words of S. P. Mohanty, "representing history becomes a complex act of understanding its pluralities; the problem of representing history dissolves into the pattern whereby we organize and make sense of it, subsuming picture into process, figure into the activity of figuration itself" (1982, 41). The close analysis of the film's diverse narrative strata will reveal the overall direction of its historical argument and the varied symbolic requirements that derive from it.

In treating the film-text in this fashion, care will be taken to fully explain the narrative and historiographic theories that form the backbone of this study. In combining these three perspectives — narrative theory, historiography, and the analysis of the film-text — a uniquely productive analytic method is obtained, which, I believe, is able to penetrate and describe the text in all its density.

CHAPTER ONE

The Modeling of History:
Current Theories

The discourse of narrative fiction and the discourse of history, long thought
to be discrete domains, have been shown to possess many of the same discursive features. As Ricoeur has argued, they share the same "ultimate referent." The distinction between imaginary events and real events, which
would seemingly create an absolute division between narrative fiction
and history, is dissolved, in Ricoeur's view, by their mutual involvement
with the structures of time, which alone give meaning to events, whether
fictional or actual. Indeed, the study of the writing of history, in some
of its most advanced versions, has in effect become the study of the narrative art of history — the analysis of the rhetorical and narrative models
that inform its composition, as exemplified in the work of White and
Ricoeur. Taken in this light, a work of historical fiction, such as *1900*, can
illuminate the strategies of symbolic representation that structure both
history and fiction; it produces what might be called an aesthetic knowledge
of the past that can, if we accept the theories of White, Ricoeur, and Jameson, provide a powerful model for historical representation in general.

The Tropological Deep Structure of Hayden White

Perhaps the most impressive and radical approach to history as an
aesthetic text can be found in the work of Hayden White, whose project
is the analysis of the tropological patterns underlying different, specific
types of historical writing. In two books, entitled *Metahistory* (1973) and
Tropics of Discourse (1978), White argues that a linguistic substrate informs all historical writing and historical consciousness: "Histories (and

philosophies of history as well) . . . contain a deep structural content which is generally poetic, and specifically linguistic, in nature" (1973, ix). The interpretive act involved in historical writing is based less on the empirical data, White argues, than on aesthetic and linguistic models, intuited by historians and applied to the course of real events. The "proof" lies in the extreme diversity of "style" among various historians. Even while writing about the same events at roughly the same time, which should yield similar appraisals of the significance of events, historians apprehend the events very differently:

> In order to relate these different styles to one another as elements of a single tradition of historical thinking, I have been forced to postulate a deep level of consciousness on which a historical thinker chooses conceptual strategies by which to explain or represent his data. On this level, I believe, the historian performs an essentially *poetic* act, in which he *prefigures* the historical field and constitutes it as a domain . . . to explain "what was really happening" in it. This type of prefiguration may, in turn, take a number of forms, the types of which are characterizable by the linguistic modes in which they are cast. (White 1973, x)

According to White, the four principal linguistic or rhetorical modes that inform the writing of history are Metaphor, Metonymy, Synecdoche, and Irony. These same four figures, he notes, were proposed by the Renaissance philosopher Vico as the "logic" of all "poetic wisdom" (1973, 32).

Insofar as these four principal forms of figurative representation seem to be innate features of language, they are also innate features of consciousness. Reading the historical text through the linguistic theories of Jakobson and Saussure and the psychoanalysis of Piaget and Lacan, White argues that the features of the historical imagination of a particular society can be readily perceived: text and mind illuminate one another, for they emerge from the same deep linguistic structure. The historical imagination of a society, or an epoch, is thus placed on display in its choice of rhetorical forms to represent its past: "In short, the theory of Tropes provides us with a basis for classifying the deep structural forms of the historical imagination in a given period of its evolution" (31).

This four-part rhetorical scheme, for White, constitutes a deep structural matrix, a kind of primary, linguistic core that underlies cognitive processes and animates all representational schemas. As White insists, however, these are *prefigurative* strategies that must be revealed or reconstituted in the work of analysis. Historical writing also makes use of related but secondary aesthetic strategies in order to obtain the desired effect of a "realistic" explanation of the past. Among the surface textual structures that imprint a discernable (and authoritative) pattern on the course of ordinary events is "the mode of emplotment." Borrowing from Northrop Frye a taxonomy of archetypal story forms, White finds historical narratives falling rather neatly into one of four main categories: Romance, Comedy, Tragedy, and Satire. While there is some variety and mixing of modes of emplotment in the individual historical text, in the main it will adhere to one of these major categories. This is primarily because of "restrictions" on historiographic form: "Historical stories tend to fall into the categories elaborated by Frye precisely because the historian is inclined to resist construction of the complex peripeteias which are the novelist's and the dramatist's stock in trade. Precisely because the historian is not (or claims not to be) telling the story 'for its own sake,' he is inclined to emplot his stories in the most conventional forms" (8).

Michelet, for example, casts his histories in the form of the Romance genre, which is characterized by the striving of an individual hero against the forces of the world opposing him. The typical conflicts the individual protagonist experiences, and triumphantly resolves, can be thematized as good against evil, virtue against vice, light against darkness, and so on: "The Romance is fundamentally a drama of self identification symbolized by the hero's transcendence of the world of experience, his victory over it, and his final liberation from it—the sort of drama associated with the Grail legend or the story of the resurrection of Christ in Christian mythology" (8). Other historians draw from different literary paradigms for their mode of emplotment; Ranke, in White's view, casts his stories in the Comic mode, with Comedy understood as promoting the reconciliation of natural and social forces. "In Comedy, hope is held out for the temporary triumph of man over his world by the prospect of occasional reconciliation of the forces at play in the social and natural worlds. Such reconciliations are symbolized in the festive occasions which the Comic writer traditionally uses to terminate his dramatic accounts of change and transformation" (9). Similarly, Tragedy can be recognized in the histories of Tocqueville, and Irony and Satire in those of Burckhardt. The principal characteristic of the Tragic form, insofar as it relates to historiographic models, is that the law governing the affairs of men is made visible through its frustration of the designs of men. The "fall of the protagonist" is accompanied by a certain gain in understanding: "And this gain is thought to consist in the epiphany of the law governing human existence which the protagonist's exertions against the world have brought to pass" (9). According to White, Marx's is a Tragic vision of the historical process, although the culmination of the historical process—the end of history—is seen as comic (10). Finally, the Satiric or Ironic mode, which points to the futility and delusory nature of any patterned perception of the world, is the prevailing form of modern historiography. It is no less "plotted," however, than the other three schemas, for it refers to them implicitly and explicitly: "stories cast in the Ironic mode, of which Satire is the fictional form, gain their effects precisely by frustrating normal expectations about the kinds of resolutions provided by stories cast in other modes" (8).

Two other strategies that structure the writing of history are discerned by White: the "explanation by formal argument," and the "explanation by ideological implication." The former refers to cognitive operations, the latter to ethical or moral presuppositions. Taken together, these three textual strategies—mode of emplotment (Romance, Comedy, etc.), formal argument, and ideological implication—comprise the "style" of the historiographic investigation. This style can best be characterized, at the deep structural level, by way of the major tropes adumbrated above. To demonstrate how these interact in a way that reveals a determinative tropological patterning, I will concentrate on White's readings of Marx's analysis of the historical process, which he labels *Metonymic.*

By Metonymic, White means a figurative strategy by which cause and effect are interchangeable, and in which a part of an entity is related to a part of a different entity. Metonymy, for White, is a dividing operation: "Marx apprehended the historical field in the Metonymical mode. His categories of prefiguration were the categories of schism, division and alienation" (28). Corresponding to this atomized world is the dramatic structure of Tragedy. Marx, however, emplotted history according to two contrary dramatic schemas, Tragedy and Comedy, discerning a twofold movement in the historical process:

> for Marx, history had to be emplotted in two ways simultaneously, in the mode of Tragedy and in the mode of Comedy. For although man *lives* Tragically, inasmuch as his attempts to construct a viable human community are continually frustrated by the laws that govern history while he remains in the social state, he also lives Comically, insofar as this interaction between Man and society progressively moves man toward a condition in which society will be dissolved and a genuine community, a communistic mode of existence, will be constituted as his true historic identity." (287)

This *aesthetic* conception of the historical process is complicated further by the cognitive process, or "mode of explanation" Marx employed to analyze the sociohistorical reality. White divides these modes of explanation into four types: Organicist, Formist, Mechanistic, and Contextualist, which are combined, in certain restricted aggregations, with the aesthetic mode of emplotment. Marx in general argued a Mechanistic explanation of historical process. He sought to expose the overarching laws and principles of history, looking at individual phenomena (i.e., social systems, social conflicts) as manifestations of these ineluctable laws:

> The Mechanistic theory of explanation turns upon the search for the causal laws that determine the outcomes of processes discovered in the historical field. The objects that are thought to inhabit the historical field are construed as existing in the modality of part-part relationships, the specific configurations of which are determined by the laws that are presumed to govern their interactions. Thus a Mechanist such as Buckle, Taine, Marx, or . . . even Tocqueville, studies history in order to divine the laws that actually govern its operations and *writes* history in order to display a narrative form the effects of those laws. (17)

The Tragic mode of emplotment works in concert with the Mechanistic mode of argument, insofar as Tragedy reveals the ineluctable laws that govern the affairs of men. But the Comic mode of emplotment, in which history is ultimately seen as a liberation, an instrument of redemption, is, in Marx, incompatible with a Mechanistic explanation. Comedy implies an overcoming of the limits placed on human relationships by the reality of social life, limits that reveal themselves as laws in the Mechanistic mode of argumentaion. Thus, the bivalent emplotment of history that Marx fashions necessitates two different models of cognitive explanation, as well. This difference, this dual modeling system, in manifest in Marx's programmatic differentiation between the Base and the Superstructure: "When Marx said that his conception of history was 'dialectical-materialistic,' what he meant was that he conceived the processes of the Base of society mechanistically and the processes of the Superstructure Organicistically. This combination alone permitted him to believe that, over the long run, a structure of human relationships that is essentially extrinsic and mechanical in nature can eventuate in a qualitatively different structure, instrisic and organismic in the way it relates parts to wholes" (286). By Organicistic, White means a mode of explanation that looks for the unifying, integrative principles linking separate historical phenomena, usually in a microcosmic-macrocosmic relation. This type of Organicist explanation generally posits an end point, or goal, to which historical processes are tending. This *telos*, however, is seen as a potential fulfillment of human destiny, rather than as a set of limitations on human progress, as in the Mechanistic mode: "In fact, for the Organicist, such (unifying) principles and ideas function not as restrictions on the human capacity to realize a distinctively human goal in history, as the 'laws' of history can be supposed to do in the thought of the Mechanist, but as guarantors of an essential human freedom" (16).

23

Thus the Mechanistic explanation of the Base involves a mode of emplotment that is linear and essentially synchronic: "On the level of the Base, there is nothing but a succession of distinctive means of production and of the modes of their relationships, a succession that is governed by strict causal laws similar to those that obtain in nature" (286). These laws are unchanging, and thus admit to a synchronic form of analysis. On the level of the Superstructure, however, an evolutionary pattern is discerned by Marx, leading to an ultimate Comic reconciliation: "On the superstructural level, by contrast, the *progressus* consists of a deepening of human consciousness' perception of man's alienation from himself and from his fellow man and a corresponding development of the social conditions within which that alienation can be transcended" (286).

These three strategies — mode of emplotment (aesthetic), mode of argument (cognitive), and mode of ideological implication (Marx's radical program) — which together give form and coherence to an explanation of historical reality, are founded on a dual tropological conception. In Marxian thought the tension between the recognition of a divided world and the certainty of a future unified one, between the Tragic and the Comic narrative course of history, between determinative and redemptive views, originates at the prefigurative level, according to White, as a tension between Metonymic and Synecdochic modes of apprehension. Synecdoche is here understood as an operation relating parts to wholes, in contrast to Metonymy, which relates part to part; Synecdoche is thus an integrative rather than a splintering operation. White insists that this "deep structure" has primacy in any act of historical explanation: "the historian confronts the historical field in much the same way that a grammarian might confront a new language . . . the historian's problem is to construct a linguistic protocol . . . In the poetic act which precedes the formal analysis of the field, the historian both creates his object of analysis and predetermines the modality of the conceptual strategies he will use to explain it" (30–31).

The essential difficulty in Marx's writing thus centers around the problem of how to integrate these two prefigurative strategies, the Metonymic and the Synecdochic. White goes so far as to say that the major issues turn on linguistic considerations: "The essence of Marx's thought about history, its structures and processes, consists less in an attempt to combine what he thought was valid in the thought of Hegel, Feurbach, the British Political Economists, and the Utopian Socialists, than in his effort to synthesize the tropological patterns of Metonymy and Synecdoche in a comprehensive image of the historical world" (285). This picture of the world, framed and organized by a kind of prior linguistic processing, is characterized by a shifting movement between two points of view: "Marx's thought moved between Metonymical apprehensions of the severed condition of mankind in its social state and Synecdochic intimations of the unity he spied at the end of the world historical process" (285). The manner in which they are synthesized, according to White, involves a shift in the mode of emplotment, making the Tragic a mere phase within the overall Comic process of history; it is ultimately by referring to the mode of emplotment, to dramatic categories, that Marx conceives a synthesis. And this shift in dramatic configurations is our evidence of what might be called a geological shift in the deep linguistic structure as well.

Tropological Structures in *1900*

Bertolucci's *1900* is conceived in very similar terms, as a Marxian history struggling with two competing modes of emplotment. Here the juxtaposition of Comic and Tragic dramatic forms is made explicit in the film's two models of the historical process. The collective life of the peasants is associated with the Comic mode, and theirs is the controlling historical vision at the end of the film. The Tragic mode, on the other hand, is clearly present in the film in the story of the bourgeoisie, whose dominant position and fall from power is closely chronicled. The notion of the Tragic as a mere phase within the overall Comic structure of history is well illustrated in the last two scenes. Here the utopian moment that had been anticipated throughout the film manifests itself in the form of a peasant celebration, a Comic "festive occasion" signaling the transformation of the old order. This in turn gives way to an explicit visualization of the merging of separate moments of time in the lives of the characters. The world historical process is quite clearly seen as a Comic one, a point that is reinforced by the association of the peasants not only with the Comic but also with the future. As Bertolucci says: "But the thing that counts is that April 25 comes tomorrow, not yesterday. It's made like a prophecy, not a chronicle" (1977, 17). The film implies that the historical process will end in a form of triumphant collectivity, "a reconciliation of forces in the social and natural worlds."

A Tragic vision is embodied within this overall Comic one, however, in the story of the bourgeoisie. The film splits its focalization between the peasantry and the bourgeois class, and thus projects two competing views of the historical process. The story of the Berlinghieris corresponds to the Tragic mode in a variety of ways. Most of all, the laws governing human affairs seem to be made visible by the failures of Alfredo, the "liberal" landowner. Not only is he unable to effect an enlightened regime, but his complicity with the Fascists, which seems to have its source in sexual insecurity, plays out a familiar design, the decline of a class that can maintain its hegemony only by force. The epiphany of overarching human law that the film conveys can be seen in the determining role class plays in forging Alfredo's tragic character. Despite his early resistance to violent measures against the peasantry, he conforms to the typical role of the Padrone the moment he takes power, highlighting the absolute nature of class identity. The Tragic outcome of the bourgeoisie, which is seen passing into historical oblivion, is only one phase, however, in the film's longer view of the historical process, which is governed by the Comic mode.

Thus White's reading allows us to correlate Marx's view of the dramatic structure of the historical process with Bertolucci's. In both, there is a similar split mode of apprehension, Comic and Tragic.

Limitations of White's "Metahistory"

The modeling system devised by White passes over some of the most crucial issues in historiography. He assumes the comparability of fiction and history, for example, without considering how history becomes textualized in the first place. Simply claiming an insight into a particular historian's poetic or linguistic predispositions is not enough to account for such a vast intertextual process as historical modeling. Both the notion of the text and the notion of history are profoundly intertextual and trans-individual, and to approach this problem by way of the poetic apprehension of the individual historian is in no way a sufficient mechanism for describing the process by which the real event becomes transformed by the web of textual practices.

Secondly, when writing on Marx, White stresses the mode of emplotment as corresponding to the deep historical structure. The narrative structuration of Marx's historiography is thus implicitly endorsed. The question of narrative form is a much-contested issue in historiography, and White's uncritical acceptance of the deep-structural status of the mode of emplotment (visible in his treatment of Marx) fails to provide a rationale for the comparison of history and narrative except on the most obvious level of affinity.

Jameson, for one, critiques White on exactly this point, claiming that his emphasis on the tropic deep structure is really a reduction of surface linguistic features to an underlying generative principle that is itself merely a camouflaged narrative system: "even if this underlying system is described in terms of 'master tropes' which organize surface tropes or figures, the status of such master tropes must ultimately be sought in a wholly different system altogether. My own experience suggests this second or 'deep' system can always be grasped and rewritten in terms of something like a narrative or teleological vision of history" (1988, 169).

For Claude Lévi-Strauss, for example, the typical distinction claimed for the narrativized text of history — that it adheres to an order already present in the world, and that this order is merely recorded, like an impression taken in soft wax, by the historian — is utterly fallacious: the notion of historical continuity and coherence that is propounded in the historical account is merely a "fraudulent outline" imposed upon events. Any image of coherence that the account achieves is the coherence of myth, rather than of "actuality": "In spite of worthy and indispensable efforts to bring another moment in history alive and to possess it, a clairvoyant history should admit that it never completely escapes from the nature of myth" (1963, 36; also in White 1973, 102). Under the impact of the structuralist model, the text of history and the text of fiction, the legal text and the biblical passage, are all susceptible to the same form of analysis.

Whether this represents a productive development cannot be argued here; what it does entail is a radical reconceptualization of the basic boundaries or lines of demarcation between textual orders — partitions that have long been held inviolate. Thomas Pavel writes that in the West in general, there are three such textual boundaries or lines of demarcation that cannot be transmigrated. In his terminology, these consist of "Sacred borders, actuality borders, and representational borders" (Pavel 1981). These boundaries are not clear-cut, although they evidently manifest completely different ontological properties. As "conventional frames," they are absolute although unmarked divisions of the conceptual field. Now the pursuit of what Lévi-Strauss calls a "clairvoyant history" would seem to demand a transmigration across these conventional boundaries. One way of treating history with reference to these conventional frames would be to see it as a kind of hinge, or intersection, between these orders, with a specifically "clairvoyant" history involving a back and forth movement between the actual, the representational, and the sacred or, better, the visionary or prophetic. Another means of relating history to these borders, or domains, is the tack taken by White in his critique of conventional historiography. There is a sense in which White's dissatisfaction with conventional historiography can be seen as a reaction against what he sees as a mixing of textual orders. Traditional historiography believes itself to be working within the frame of the actual, rather than the representational, failing to see the permeability of these orders and bringing to the manifestly representational arts of history the pretense of actuality. By confusing the order of the representational with that of the actual, traditional historiography condemns itself to a blind, Quixotic pursuit of a referent whose "reality" becomes all the more hallucinatory when its status as a representation is denied.

Historical writing was not always regarded as indentured to reality, however, and in early periods the common basis of historical and poetic writing was recognized. The mixture of imaginative and documentary writing was seen not only as unavoidable, given the tropological bedrock of all discourse, but desirable, as it allowed access to a higher form of truth. The dominant opposition was not between "truth" and "fiction," as it has come to be seen in the nineteenth and twentieth centuries, but between truth and error: fiction could be as much a species of "truth" as documentary writing. Historians of an earlier age, according to White, implicitly recognized that the imaginative ingredient of historical discourse did not diminish its validity: "Prior to the French Revolution, historiography was conventionally regarded as a literary art. More specifically, it was regarded as a branch of rhetoric and its 'fictive' nature generally recognized . . . they did not on the whole view historiography as a representation of the facts unalloyed by elements of fancy . . . Truth was not equated with fact, but with a combination of fact and the conceptual matrix within which it was appropriately located in the discourse. The imagination no less than the reason has to be engaged in any adequate representation of the truth" (1978, 123).

History without a Subject or a *Telos*: The Historiography of Louis Althusser

The disavowal of the "art" of history in favor of a definition of it as "science" is common in current historiography. Even where historiography traditionally claims a preeminent position as a "totalizing perspective," as in Marxian thought, we find a striking distrust of its larger, visionary potential. Louis Althusser, for example, identifies history with science in the most explicit terms, characterizing each as a "process which has no real subject and goals." Both science and history are described as impersonal and without a *telos*. Both science and history "impose a subjectless system of representation on the world" (Bennett 1979, 119). Indeed, this mirror identification of history and science is crucial to Althusser's definition of science (composing, along with ideology and politics, the "trilogy of the superstructure"), for the foundation of Marxian science lies precisely in its new analysis of history: "Althusser argues that it is in this sense that Marx transformed

Hegel's concept of history. Whereas Hegel conceived of history as an evolutionary process which is governed, given sense and coherence by the concept of history as a 'process without a subject . . .' Marx thus made the study of history scientific, not because he claimed to know the 'truth' of history, as had earlier philosophies of history, but precisely the opposite, because he made history problematic" (Bennett 1979; 120).

Now this proclamation of history as science seems hopelessly at odds with the literary apprehension of history argued by Hayden White. For Althusser, there can be no real intercourse between literature and history conceived as a science. Literature, which occupies an aesthetic "middle ground" between science and ideology, works upon the same object as science, i.e., the Real, but gives us the Real in a very different form and with very different instruments: "The real difference between art and science lies in the specific form in which they give us the same object in quite different ways: art in the form of 'seeing' and 'perceiving' or 'feeling,' science in the form of *knowledge* (in the strict sense, by concepts)" (Althusser 1971). Art works upon the Real by revealing its ideological encoding and thus produces a "knowledge" somewhat comparable to science. This is not quite a "knowledge effect," for art does not provide us with a knowledge of "class determination," but it does produce an "aesthetic effect," which consists of making visible the real fact of ideology. Art occupies an equivocal position, however, and is ultimately subjected to an ideological reinscription, a covering over of the gaps and fissures it has disclosed. No such ideological reinscription occurs in Althusser's version of science, which is aligned in opposition to ideology, for the knowledge it produces is precisely destructive of the imaginary mis-recognitions of the ideological.

Althusser's elevation of these epistemological categories — science, literature, ideology — to a level approaching sovereign status, with each category jealously guarding its own frontiers, has been roundly criticized; yet the ultimate target of both his critics and Althusser himself remains the same — historicism, the "stages" theory of history with its "periodizing" and "evolutionist" program. The proper analysis of history, for Althusser, begins with the recognition that the "real object" cannot be known; the temporal unfolding of events belongs to the order of the referent, to the order of the Real, which resists symbolization and therefore cannot be reflected in the scientific model. What can be known is the "object of knowledge:" "What has to be respected is the rigorous distinction between the *real object* and the concept of *object of knowledge* so as to stay on the razor's edge without veering off 'to the left' into empiricism or 'to the right' into formalism" (Balibar 1977). History, which is neither the unmediated events nor the large-scale narrative patterning discerned in evolutionist histories, is seen as an "absent cause." It can be known only through its effects at various sites in the social and cultural system, and can be known only through the kind of science that favors synchronic analyses. Althusser assimilates history to the synchronic concept of the "mode of production," which can be understood as a kind of abstraction and enlargement of the traditional Marxian concept of the Base. The mode of production subsumes all of the semiautonomous practices of economics, law, science and ideology: "the properly Marxian notion of an all-embracing and all-structuring mode of production (which assigns everything within itself — culture, ideological production, class articulation, technology — a specific and unique place)" (Jameson 1981, 90). Yet, as an absent cause, the mode of production is not a tangible entity: it is seen simply as the dynamic interrelationships within the synchronic structure, interrelationships that act upon one another through the energy of the invisible cause that formulates them into a total system: "Althusser's Marxism . . . is a structuralism for which only *one* structure exists: namely, the mode of production itself, or the synchronic system of social relations as a whole. This is the sense in which this 'structure' is an absent cause, since it is nowhere empirically present as an element, it is not a part of the whole or one of the levels, but rather the entire system of *relationships* among those levels" (Jameson 1981, 36).

The mode of production can be seen as a substitute for the epistemological priority assumed by history in earlier Marxian theory. It is, in effect, an attempt at a nontropological, nonnarrative, nondiachronic history: a history focused on present effects. "The organizing concept of the mode of production developed primarily in Althusser and Balibar . . . can be seen as the most advanced attempt to construct a non-evolutionist and non-empiricist Marxist theory of history . . . Historical materialism is founded on the concrete analysis of concrete situations in which the politics of the present conjuncture and the ideologically given require analysis" (Johnston 1977, 6).

White versus Althusser: The Structuralist Connection

The gulf between the positions assumed by White and Althusser could hardly be wider and seems very difficult to span. While both insist on the distance between historical representation and reality, they diverge in the different directions that this freedom from mimesis takes them. Althusser conveys his version of structuralist history to the precincts of science, with its "unmotivated" relational systems, whereas White addresses his rhetorical model to the affective level of poetic response, where history is a question of deep tropic figuration. The distance between these conceptions is most evident in their very different appraisals of Marx's approach to history. For White, Marx's historiography represents a crowning aesthetic achievement, the synthesis of two dissimilar tropes, producing a novel, bivalent scheme of history. For Althusser, on the other hand, Marxian historiography, seen in its proper light, constitutes a new science, opening up a new problematic, a new object of knowledge. These incompatible views belie the common origin of both approaches in structural linguistics, with its underlying argument for the autonomy and structuring impact of the symbolic. White, for example, emphasizes the linguistic, prefigurative apprehension of the world as a deep-structural level, prior to any other cognitive or perceptual operation, thus highlighting the interaction of what Saussure called "langue" and "parole" in the articulation of reality. Emphasizing different elements of Saussurean theory, Althusser places the stress on synchronic analysis, implicitly adopting Saussure and Hjelmslev's insistence that "the explanation of a present state is not to be sought in a past state of the same thing," and adopts as a methodological principle the linguistic rule that "diachrony does not explain synchrony" (Nowell-Smith 1977, 9). Althusser identifies the total social system with a kind of language order, conceiving it as synchronic, and, like language, as an autonomous system that is not dependent on, or even closely tied to, the referent, the actual object. Again, the distinction between the actual object and the object of knowledge discussed above can be related directly to the Saussurean "bracketing" of the referent.

Fredric Jameson and the Text of History

The synthesis of these two divergent approaches is the signal accomplishment of Frederic Jameson in *The Political Unconscious*. By approaching history through its "prior textualizations," Jameson "completes" the Althusserian dictum that history is an absent cause:

> What Althusser's own insistence on history as an absent cause makes clear, but what is missing from the formula as it is canonically worded, is that he does not at all draw the fashionable conclusion that because history is a text, the 'referent' does not exist. We should therefore propose the following revised formulation: that history is not a text, not a narrative, master or otherwise, but that, as an absent cause, it is inaccessible to us except in textual form, and that our approach to it and to the Real itself necessarily passes through its prior textualization, its narrativization in the political unconscious. (1981, 35)

31

In offering a vision of history as palimpsest, Jameson effectively conflates the tropological and the scientific approaches to history. It can be known "conceptually," but only by passing through a textual layer, a kind of atmospheric or gravitational field, which the particular conjuncture of the present makes visible. Most importantly, this concept represents a way of synthesizing the Althusserian concentration on the synchronic mode of production with the older Marxian diachronic history of stages or periods — the "evolutionist" theory of history that Jameson insists on retaining, specifically for its utopian destination.

The actual paradigm underpinning Marxian historicism has been badly understood, Jameson argues. The traditional Marxian narrative of history is more properly considered a "genealogy," a distinction Nietzsche was the first to draw. Althusser seems both party and exception to this misapprehension. Critics conventionally point out, for instance, that in Marxian evolutionary history, earlier forms of production are mistakenly seen to "grow into" capitalism, to evolve unidirectionally, and to bear within them a genetic predisposition to a system to which they logically bear no relation. Jameson counters that this is not the view developed in *Capital* of diachronic succession; rather, the model is that of the genealogy: "In genealogical construction, we begin with a full blown system (capitalism in Marx) in terms of which elements of the past can 'artificially' be isolated as objective preconditions: genealogy is not a historical *narrative*, but has the essential function of renewing our perception of the synchronic system as in an X-ray, its diachronic perspectives serving to make perceptible the articulation of the functional elements of a given system in the present" (1981, 139). In the genealogical model, the situations of the past must be integrated into an account of the present, not to show "how we arrived," but to expose the "functional" elements of the present.

Crucial to this operation of genealogical reconstruction is a refined conception of the mode of production, one which adds a diachronic perspective to Althusser's total synchronic system. Within any dominant mode of production, Jameson argues, there exist several remnants or residues of earlier modes, practices or beliefs dating from earlier periods that survive into the present. An example might be the persistence of patriarchal modes of behavior, a vestige of the earliest modes of production, in capitalist society, where these concepts and types of relations no longer function instrumentally. The mode of production is not, therefore, a monolithic and uniform total system, but a complex lamination of different social realities, different period practices. Expanding on the idea of the "social formation" proposed by Nicos Poulantzis (basically, a concrete "social" version of the abstract concept of the mode of production), Jameson characterizes the mode of production as a layered composite, displaying different historical strata:

> every social formation or historically existing society has in fact consisted in the overlay and structural coexistence of *several* modes of production all at once, including vestiges and survivals of older modes . . . historical epochs are not monolithically integrated social formations, but on the contrary, complex overlays of different modes of production which serve as the bases of different social groups and classes. It is because there are a number of different modes of production in any given historical epoch that different classes can exist in a variety of kinds of antagonism with one another. (1981, 95)

History and Aesthetic Form

The survival and coexistence of older forms of social life are best represented in the work of art; it is both universal, all-embracing, and determined by the sociohistorical conjuncture from which it emerges: it is the form that best displays both the continuity of cultures and epochs and the radical disparateness and "time-bound" nature of earlier cultural situations. Conceived on the model of the social formation summarized above, the artistic artifact appears as a layered, multi-storied discourse, embodying several different modes of production within it. These older modes of production are discernible in the artifact in the form of generic conventions and aesthetic paradigms, the formal language of the work, which is intertextually derived from various periods. Each generic configuration incorporated in the composite form that is the artifact bears the imprint of the period in which it emerged as a strong form. Genres that are emergent in a particular period may be residual in a later period: "Each generic form is a contested, conflictual residue of the uses of the numerous versions of the form . . . However, there emerges something like a 'structure in dominance,' the dominant coexisting in polemic form with all its other historical possibilities" (Mohanty 1982, 40). Furthermore, each inherited, borrowed, or original genre carries its own ideological charge, its own "socio-symbolic message," as Jameson writes. Older forms sedimented within the artifact may thus constitute a kind of second voice, or competing aesthetic paradigm. The work of art, rather than being conceived as unified or singular, displays instead a "layered or marbled structure." In its mosaiclike composition (its textuality) the work of art opens directly onto history.

Dominant and Secondary Voices in *1900*

1900 displays these characteristics in its composite generic structure as well as in its narrative layering of perspectives. The most striking generic dissonance occurs in the combination of the epic form, centered on the character Olmo and his deeds on behalf of the peasantry, and the psychological, novelistic narrative form that details the life of the character Alfredo and his ambivalent, self-destructive behavior. Where Olmo is perceived with a clarity unshadowed by psychological nuance, almost wholly defined by his heroic role, Alfredo is drawn with a heavy chiaroscuro of psychological complexity and neurosis that comes into focus through his inability to navigate between his role as Padrone, which he embodies in an especially cruel fashion, and the occasionally revealed deeper sensitivity of the character, expressed mainly in his passion for his wife and for his friend Olmo.

The result of this dissonance is the juxtaposition of two strikingly different storytelling modes: the messages these generic configurations emit could not be more opposed. Where the epic form historically expresses an early, ideal state, chronicling the deeds of a hero and a people in the process of forming a collective, unified identity, the psychological, novelistic form in which Alfredo's story is told has as one of its chief themes the notion of alienation: the ineradicable gap between individual desire and collective purpose. This discordant combination seen in these competing "socio-symbolic messages" can be related to the different modes of production depicted in the film: the precapitalist mode of the peasants versus the capitalist mode, with its remnants of feudal production, displayed in the fading life of the Padrone. The generic codes of the film open onto history in this fashion, as the text itself contains different strong forms that bear the imprint of different periods of time. The survival of older forms of social life within the capitalist mode of production is here emblematized, not simply in the collective existence of the peasantry, but, just as significantly, in the epic form used to articulate their struggle. As a side note, one could relate this issue to the interesting failure of one of Bertolucci's ideas for the end of the film. Originally, he planned to mark the advent of a new order at the end of the work by giving to the peasants the cameras, microphones — the entire cinematic apparatus. The Communist mode of production would, in a sense, be represented through the "popular," vernacular cinematic techniques of the peasants, recording one another in the midst of their celebration. Bertolucci has said that the results were interesting but unwatchable. While this type of popular cinema may not be the best representation of the future Communist mode of production, one sees in Bertolucci's attempt the effort to link aesthetics to a socio-symbolic message and to relate the larger generic form, in turn, to different modes of production.

The representation of history thus finds its model in the aesthetic object. The work of art manifests the type of dual orientation toward the past and toward the present that is required of historical representation; the dilemma of representing the past from the perspective of the present is to some degree resolved in this model of sedimented forms:

> But if this suggestion is valid, then the problem of the 'synchronic' system and of the typological temptation are both solved at one stroke. What is synchronic is the 'concept' of the mode of production; the moment of the historical coexistence of several modes of production is not synchronic in this sense, but opens to history in a dialectical way. The temptation to classify texts according to the appropriate mode of production is thereby removed, since the texts emerge in a space in which we may expect them to be criss-crossed and intersected by a variety of impulses from contradictory modes of cultural production all at once. (Jameson 1981, 95)

The Prestidigitation of Narrative Form

It is narrative art specifically that exemplifies the intersection of the historical and the textual. Jameson confers upon narrative a privileged mediatory status: "the specific critical and interpretive task [is] . . . to restructure the problematics of ideology, of the unconscious and of desire, of representation, of history and of cultural production, around the all-informing process of narrative, which I take to be (here using the short-hand of philosophical idealism) the central function or instance of the human mind" (1981, 13). Narrative achieves this singular status purely by its formal properties, its logic of combination and juxtaposition, its staging of conflict and resolution — reminiscent of the way the mind, confronted with a problem, will try out a series of logical solutions. Narrative is privileged for its ability to project imaginary solutions in symbolic form to real social contradictions, contradictions that are repressed and surface only in coded or symbolic form. Narrative, however, does not simply *reflect* the heterogeneous perspectives of social life, the composite and variegated structures of the mode of production, but *reformulates* the patterns of conflict it discovers, *restructuring* the ideological contradictions that trouble and disturb the social formation.

This "prestidigitation" of narrative does not work directly upon the real, however, for the text cannot operate upon a prelinguistic field, it cannot effect meaning from that which is asymbolic. Rather it works upon the already textualized level Jameson calls the "ideologeme." The ideologeme is kind of subatomic article of ideology—the "minimal unit of class discourse," which expresses itself in various ways, in the form of a value-system for example, or a philosophical construct, or a protonarrative fantasy. The ideologeme can be seen as the "ideologically charged raw material" (Mohanty 1982, 37) that the narrative process orchestrates into new patterns. Narrative is seen then as a process, a generative principle, rather than as a fixed form.

The representation of history then becomes, once again, a question of tropological figuration—textual strategies—with the crucial difference that what is modeled by these tropological operations is already an extremely complex "text": "representing history becomes a complex act of understanding its pluralities; the problem of representing history dissolves into the pattern whereby we organize and make sense of it, subsuming picture into process, figure into the activity of figuration itself" (Mohanty 1982, 41).

The "meaning" of history resides then not in its teleology, nor in its appeal to a prediscursive level of reality, but, to a large degree, in the very process of transcoding from one level to another, of translating from one text to another—the process that contemporary linguistic theory finds constitutive of meaning itself. In this fashion, history (seen as a series of prior textualizations,) comes to resemble the movement of semiosis. Quoting Algirdas Greimas on this point, Jameson maintains that significance is "nothing but . . . transposition from one level of language to another, from one language to a different language, and meaning is nothing but the possibility of such transcoding" (1972, 215–16). Historical meaning emerges then in a kind of cubistic multiplication of discursive registers; the operation of the text comes to resemble the interaction of the multiple "effects" posited by structural causality: the functioning of the text of history becomes a kind of translation of the operations of the mode of production.

Hindess and Hirst

"History as semiosis"—the ultimate conclusion of this argument, places a very different burden on the strategic representation of the past, a burden that is not teleological, surely, nor mindlessly referential, but one that is equally limiting and strictured. This extreme conclusion is emblematically and powerfully presented in the work of Hindess and Hirst entitled *Pre-Capitalist Modes of Production*. Articulating a position that Althusser himself refused to assume, Hindess and Hirst argue that because history is only a series of texts, as such it cannot exist. According to this view, the past is merely a body of texts, documents selected in the present for the purpose of ideological investment: "Far from working on the *past*, the ostensible object of history, historical knowledge works on a body of *texts*. These texts are a product of historical knowledge. The writing of history is the production of texts which interpret these texts." Furthermore, "the object of history is whatever is represented as having hitherto existed" (Hindess and Hirst 1975, 309–11).

Jameson resists this ultimate structuralist position by stressing the conceptual importance of the past as a kind of precondition for a notion of the future. He also points out that the "proper articulation" of a concrete mode of production *necessarily entails the projection of all the other modes* that coexist within it (1988, 176), foregrounding the fact of historical difference, of the complicated overlay of different periods and structures that make up the present moment, the nonsynchronous development of different practices.

The Genealogical Model

Apprehended thus genealogically, or better, archaeologically, the past is seen strictly in terms of how it is different from the present, rather than, as in Hindess and Hirst, complicit with the present, and inextricable from the ideological needs of the present. Thus an authentic knowledge of the past can be gained, a knowledge that dialectically educates us about the present. Restored to its significant difference, the past "will come before us as a radically different life form which rises up to call our own form of life into question and to pass judgment on it . . . it is not we who sit in judgment on the past, but rather the past, the radical difference of other modes of production, which judges us, imposing the painful knowledge of what we are not, what we are no longer, what we are not yet" (Jameson 1988, 175).

Not only the past, but the *future* as well sits in judgment on the present. The genealogical model, according to Jameson, also implies a future mode of production; it projects the potential for radical change, rather than presuming a steady state: if "the proper articulation of any concrete mode of production structurally implies the projection of all other conceivable modes, then it follows that it implies the future as well" (Jameson 1988, 176).

The comprehension of the past in terms of narrative understanding involves another kind of causality, what White in an article on Jameson called narratological causality: "the seizing of a past by consciousness in such a way as to make of the present a fulfillment rather than an effect of some prior (mechanistic, expressive, or structural) cause" (White 1987, 149). Here, one of the central characteristics of narrative is extrapolated as a model of historical causality: the notion that early events contain the seeds of later developments, although the early events may not be visible until a certain perspective is attained. Rather than a conclusive order, fixed and immobile, the past contains, in germinal or perhaps virtual form, a range of incipient, alternative practices and events.

Seen as a "prefiguration of a project to be realized in some future" the narrativization of the past can serve as the basis for a specific kind of historical action. A society, or an individual, may elect to substitute another, different past for that past from which it had actually descended. In the view of White and Jameson, this genealogical approach, which derives from Nietzsche, manifestly affects the actual historical past; when a revolutionary society, for example, undertakes to rewrite its history, it stresses events that had previously been seen as unimportant, but that are now understood as prefigurations or anticipations of the new social and historical order. Furthermore, these previously unmarked events are understood as a field of projects to be realized in the future, thus impelling a distinctly historical form of action. As White explains: "human beings can will backward as well as forward in time; willing backward occurs when we rearrange accounts of events in the past that have been emplotted in a given way in order to endow them with a different meaning or to draw from the new emplotment reasons for acting differently in the future . . . Insofar as we can regard this change of perspective as a causal force in history, it can be seen as effecting changes in past ages' conceptions of their natures as given in the records they produced" (1987, 150).

The process of narrative modeling thus provides a kind of imaginative or aesthetic knowledge of the past. Contrary to Althusser's position, however, this knowledge may be seen as equal to that knowledge provided by science: "art and literature claim an authority different in kind from that claimed by both science and politics. It is the authority of 'culture' which is to be distinguished from that of 'society' precisely by the universal translatability of the forms of its products" (White 1982, 3). This universal translatability is precisely the goal of Marxian historiography, according to Jameson, for it must deal not only with "specific concrete situations," but must also situate events in the framework of "one great collective story," as "vital episodes in a single, unfinished plot." The mechanism for transcoding the specific into the universal is provided by narrative form, which is capable of linking different concrete instances to one another, and which serves as a hinge between different orders of ideology, history, and imagination.

This more complex and refined narrative model of history, what might be called a prismatic narrative as opposed to a developmental or unilinear model, is offered as an explicit endorsement of the imaginative form of knowledge proper to any form of historical recounting. As White maintains: "How else can any past, which by definition comprises events, processes, structures, and so forth, considered to be no longer perceivable, be represented in either consciousness or discourse except in an 'imaginary' way? Is it not possible that the question of narrative in any discussion of historical theory is always finally about the function of imagination in the production of a specifically human truth?" (1987, 57).

Finally, we may say that the primary accomplishment of the model Jameson provides in *The Political Unconscious* is to subsume the opposition between synchrony and diachrony in Marxian historical thought; in so doing, it also overcomes the distinction between science and literature that has been the focus of sharp debates in traditional as well as Marxian historiography.

Temporality—the Shared Referent:
The Historiography of Paul Ricoeur

Paul Ricoeur has also argued for the productive interplay of narrative and literary form and historical writing. His *Time and Narrative* is a sustained analysis of the shared features of literary and historical writing. Literature and historical writing both concern, over and above their immediate referents—imaginary events on the one hand and actual events on the other—a concentrated secondary reference to the structures of temporality. What gives historical writing its "aura of historicality," for Ricoeur, is precisely this overarching concern for the experience of time, without which history cannot go beyond the status of the chronicle. Literature, for Ricoeur, displays the same concern for the mystery of temporality; in fact, it provides deeper lessons regarding the human experience of time than does historical writing. The significance of events derives from the web of temporal relationships in which they occur; the goal of historical writing and of literature is precisely to bring into relief this "ultimate referent," which can be described only indirectly.

The structure that provides access to this ultimate referent is narrativity, or emplotment. Ricoeur argues that temporality is "the structure of existence that reaches language in narrativity" and that narrativity is "the language structure that has temporality as its ultimate referent" (1980, 169). Only narrative can deal with the mystery of time, for the comprehension of time eludes any discursive or rational framework: "speculation on time is an inconclusive rumination to which narrative activity alone can respond. Not that this activity solves the aporias . . . Emplotment . . . replies to the speculative aporia with a poetic making of something capable, certainly, of clarifying the aporia . . . but not of resolving it theoretically" (1984, 6).

Emplotment serves to situate human actions in the largest possible framework, one that can comprehend intention and contingency, forseeable consequences and intervening forces, knowable and unknowable relationships. To do justice to the full content of the historical past, history cannot be separated from lived human experience, which is set in a time dimension. The cognitive map that emplotment provides stresses, above all, the shaping influence of past events on present reality, which continue to imprint the present "long after the physical interactions which we define as past have ceased to exist" (Williams 1985, 11).

Moreover, the continuum of past, present, and future that narrativity makes perceivable is one of the cardinal functions of "historicality." Commenting on the difference between an experience of time as "mere seriality" and an experience conceived in narrative terms, White states: "In historicality, events appear not only to succeed one another in the regular order of the series but also to function as inaugurations, transitions, and terminations of processes that are meaningful because they manifest the structures of plots" (1987, 177). This type of temporal organization alone allows both a literal account of events and a secondary level of figurative meaning concerning the significance of the events, a secondary level that coincides with the meaning produced in "well-made stories."

The link between Ricoeur's concept of historicality, properly rendered through narrative, and Jameson's model of the political project uniquely facilitated by the "amplitude" and imaginative potential of narrative can be found in Ricoeur's notion of symbolic action. Narrative does not simply register the world, like an impression taken in soft wax, it refashions it:

> Narrative discourse . . . works up the material given in perception and reflection, fashions it, and creates something new, in precisely the same way that human agents by their actions fashion distinctive forms of historical life out of the world they inherit as their past . . . Historical events . . . are products of the actions of human agents seeking, more or less self-consciously, to endow the world in which they live with symbolic meaning . . . the narrativization of historical events effect a symbolic representation of the processes by which human life is endowed with symbolic meaning. (White 1987, 178).

In this notion of symbolic action that functions exactly like historical action, we find something like Jameson's concept of "narratological" causality:

a "change in perspective" as a causal force in history, facilitating a new kind of action in the past and in the future; the reformulating and restructuring of the field of the past through the perspective shifts of narrative. In both Jameson and Ricoeur historical causality is equated with symbolic action. For Jameson, it is a change in perspective; for Ricoeur it is a mode of rendering events that is "indexical" — linked to historical events through the selfsame activity and desire to endow the world with meaning. In short, historical narrative is seen as a performative discourse, a product of the same kinds of actions that produce historical events: the investing of the world with symbolic meaning.

Furthermore, Jameson and Ricoeur share a kind of providential vision that organizes the discourse. For Jameson, the historical process has a teleological orientation: the "one great collective story" in which the historical process is seen as a series of "vital episodes in a single unfinished plot" has as its end point a vision of human liberation at the end of history. Just so, Ricoeur's work points to a reality that lies beyond the historical; every great historical text not only works upon the past and provides a figuration of time, but invokes at a secondary level the struggle of humanity to get out of time, to get out of history.

Ricoeur refers to Heidegger's concept of "deep temporality" to describe this aspect of human aspiration: it is "the most authentic experience of time, that is, the dialectic of coming to be, having been, and making present. In this dialectic, time is entirely desubstantialized. The words 'future,' 'past,' and 'present' disappear, and time itself figures as the exploded unity of the three temporal extases" (1984, 61). In this unity, the goal of historical analysis can also be sought — the drive to make perceivable the way the past communicates to the present that which pertains to the future.

In the final shots of *1900*, the "exploded unity" of different temporal moments is visualized directly, as the principal characters, now old men, are returned to their childhood selves in the course of reenacting an earlier contest of courage. The rapid shuttling between present and past here invokes the future as well, for we have the distinct impression that the temporal loop can be read as a flashforward as well as a flashback. In this final scene, the various temporal strategies of the film are synthesized and condensed, and the political project of the work set within a perspective in which time is seen as a movement toward liberation, not only from political oppression but from history itself.

CHAPTER TWO

The Structure of the Plot of *1900*

Modes of Emplotment

In terms of film genres, the historical film is a very unusual hybrid, for it is defined by a discipline that is completely outside the cinema. As Pierre Sorlin points out, when speaking of the historical film it is necessary to refer both to history and to film, and to recognize that its generic identity rests upon an already constituted system of knowledge—historical knowledge—from which the film takes its material (Sorlin 1980, 20). This not only introduces a division between actual and fictional events (a division more apparent than absolute, as discussed in the preceding chapter), but also involves, in most cases, a demarcation of public and private orders. As Sorlin writes: "It is very seldom that a film does not pass from the general to the particular, and arouse interest by concentrating on individual cause" (1980, 21).

This historical order, however, provides considerably more than simply the external framework of a reference period, more than a period context in which various individual dramas are set. In the narrative organization of the historical film a conception of history is worked into the fabric of the drama, not as an external force, but as an internal mechanism that generates events, informs choices and solutions, and determines relationships in the so-called private narratives that the characters typically enact. The divergent orientations of the historical film thus coincide at the level of the mode of emplotment. Individual events and public, large-scale historical events are articulated within a single narrative line, and synthesized at the levels of plot structure, character relationships, and temporal patterning.

We may compare the mode of emplotment of the historical film to the classic realist novel as described by Lukács. Endorsing the historical value of the realist novel, Lukács maintained that both historiography and the realist novel have as their informing principle a vital totalizing perspective. The classic realist narrative is characterized by the manner in which it makes historical forces visible, especially in the way history is shown to impinge on the protagonist and the auxiliary characters of the fiction. In the novels of Sir Walter Scott, for example, history is represented through its impact on the characters. As one commentator writes: "According to Lukács, Scott fabricated plots which center on a protagonist caught between two opposing historical forces. That protagonist's personal choices thus spring from historical conflicts, until, in order to resolve them, the plot introduces purer characters exceptionally typical of the opposing historical forces. Thus the general motive truths of historical processes, including their necessary inter-relationships in a meaningful totality, are called forth by the plot just as if history had called them forth" (Rosen 1984, 26).

The movement of the narrative seems to be controlled, not by the narrator or by Scott, the author, but by the large-scale "motive truths" of history. This, at least, is the effect that the realist narrative pursues in its particular form of construction. The totalizing perspective that is achieved is a product, however, of the narrative apparatus itself: it is the plot design and the character-system that produce and generate this historical order, casting up ever more representative types, ever purer specimens, "exceptionally typical of the opposing historical forces."

Lukács's description of the historical novel stands very close to the bulk of historical films as well, from *Birth of a Nation* to *Danton*. In film, moreover, the concentration on character as a kind of "medium" of historical change is even more pronounced. In most narrative history films, there is a striking mixture of private and public events. This stems from the necessity, in film, to render history in terms that are simultaneously universal and particular. It is instructive to investigate the technique, in two different historical films, whereby singular, personal events are correlated with the wider movements of history.

In Rossellini's *Paisan*, the liberation of Italy at the end of World War II is rendered in six vignettes, focusing on the responses of ordinary people in various areas of the Peninsula. The private narratives of the protagonists enact, on a diminished scale, the international story of the destruction and reparation of Italy during the time of the liberation. In their spontaneous alliances and profound misunderstandings, in their sudden awareness of loss and the irrevocable nature of the personal change the war has wrought, the characters echo and invoke the national story. The focus on loss and the attempt at reparation that characterizes each of the six segments can be read as a concrete expression of the large-scale historical process. It is essential, in fact, to view the private narratives of the characters from this perspective: history, in the external sense of public events, is depicted only very generally, through voice-over and through an animated map showing the ongoing process of the liberation, together with a few shots of battle scenes. External history is thus dedicated only to the ruin of the opposing forces; it is left to the private narratives of the individuals to assert the hope of reconciliation and renewal.

Moreover, the film utilizes the private narratives of the characters to evoke a notion of the past itself. Each of the characters in the six vignettes relates his present experiences to his own personal history. These stories generally take the form of reminiscences, but in one case — the story of the soldier and the prostitute — an actual flashback is used: a very rare occurrence in neorealist films. Although it details a time only several months earlier, the flashback in *Paisan* is emblematic of a tendency in the film to meditate upon the past. It is the memories of the characters that serve, in fact, as the model for the film's approach to history, for it is through these memories that change, the relation of the past to the present, and the relations of the part to the whole are established. History, both personal and public, is evoked through the characters' memories — the soldier's memory of his first encounter with a woman in Rome, which he compares to the present, just six months later, when many of the women of the city have turned to prostitution; the little street orphan's memory of the bombing of the city by the American "liberators," a memory that is matched by that of his interlocutor, the black MP whose own history of poverty nearly matches that of the boy; the memory of Harriet, the American nurse in Florence, of "Lupo," formerly an artist and her lover, now the leader of the Resistance. The history *Paisan* presents is colored with the emotion of the characters' pasts, charged with subjective meaning. It is here, Rossellini implies, that history can be sought.

In the historical films of Visconti, a similar double perspective is employed. But a very different relationship between the individual and the historical process is established. The individual protagonists of *The Leopard*, *Senso*, and *Rocco and His Brothers*, for example, are seen as resistant to historical change, determined to hold on to a past order. As Geoffrey Nowell-Smith writes: "The individual and the historical are set up in conflict with one another, and the outcome of the conflict is that the individual is defeated . . . The individual — Franz, Rocco, the Prince, Gianni — rises to confront history and to be tragically defeated" (1977, 177). Rather than the individual stories mirroring the historical, as in Rossellini, the individual in Visconti reacts against history. In *The Leopard*, for example, Prince Salina is well aware of the necessity of change. Yet he insists upon maintaining a historically atavistic perspective. Rather than echoing the historical reality, he offers himself as its negation: "we wander in Prince Salina's footsteps almost throughout the whole of *The Leopard*; we are told that unity is progressing favorably, in conformity with the hopes of the king, the ruling class, and the Prince himself — but we end with the same Salina anticipating his own death: the external view (Italy in the making) is undermined by the character's subjective view" (Sorlin 1980, 55).

In *Rocco and His Brothers*, as well, the historically "backward" characters are the major protagonists of the work — Rocco, Simone, and Rosaria. They are the dramatic focus of the film, although they represent old-world morals and ideologies that are severely criticized. The character of Ciro, on the other hand, is clearly representative of the forces of progress; yet his is a dramatically insignificant role. Ironically, he is a far more significant character historically than Rocco or Rosaria. Here, too, the movement of history and the orientation of the characters are set in opposite directions.

Despite these differences, both Rossellini and Visconti effectively link the private narratives of the characters to the public world of historical consequence. At every point a double perspective is employed; the characters provide an orientation to public events through the stress laid on its impact on their personal lives. In order to effect this kind of dilation, however, the histories of the characters must have a kind of universal patterning to them. It is important to recognize the kind of dialectic set up between history and the character in the historical film. Both history and the character are charged with being particular or universal. If history is fashioned in the film as a kind of universal process, partaking of an ancient and recurrent pattern of conflict and resolution, then the character is charged with validating this conception by living out its events in a singular, particular manner. If, on the other hand, history is comprehended as particular, as a sequence of one-time events, then the character's experiences and emotions universalize it. By circulating its messages through such a self-augmenting system, the historical film attains its considerable authority and power.

In my analysis of *1900*, I will examine the way the narrative form configures, in an original way, the relations between private and public history. Rather than playing one off the other, as in Visconti, or enclosing one within the other, as in Rossellini, Bertolucci seems to advocate a composite, layered model of the historical process, in which different characters anchor different domains, each of which actualizes a certain historical reality within the aggregate structure. Here no one character or group of characters embodies the historical process, nor do any of the characters stand apart from history or rise up to confront it. Instead, the historical order contains a range of modes of production in *1900*. The bourgeois social mode, which might be called the "structure in dominance," and which is embodied in the Berlinghieri family, is crisscrossed by the survival of older forms of social life, including the peasant culture and the remnants of aristocratic, feudal social forms as well. A kind of oppositional avant-grade "culture of modernity" is also invoked and set against the tyrannical order of Fascism, which exemplifies the return of the most brutal kind of power society, usually labeled, in Marxian thought, the despotic mode of production. All of these historical realities are shown to coexist, and each is embodied in a particular character who serves as a "type." Rather than presenting a unified, singular notion of history as a current that characters either swim with or against, *1900* visualizes the historical moment as a confluence of different tributary cultures and societies, each of which emerges from a different state of historical development, and each of which has a unique perspective on historical progress and change.

In this sense, the private domain of the individual character is identified with a specific historical point of view: the motive force for individual behavior is plainly revealed to be the interference between different modes of production contained within the social formation rendered in the film. While individual psychology is apparent in the text—at no point do the characters relinquish their human dimension—the characters' psychological depth is itself historicized: the neuroses of Alfredo, the psychosis of Attila, the Fascist leader, and even the seeming submissiveness of Olmo are made historically concrete, directly linked to the conflict and struggle that defines their private and public lives.

Perhaps most importantly, the familiar "Oedipal trajectory," visible chiefly in the childhood scenes of the two protagonists, is reinvested in the historical dimension of the text, receiving very different emphases in the context of peasant as opposed to bourgeois family life. In the course of this analysis, I will argue that the early Oedipal patterning of Olmo's childhood is a necessary step in Bertolucci's elaboration of the historical process as lived by the peasants, because through it history is invested with desire, invested with a libidinal intensity that first emerges in the domain of private subjectivity. Here Olmo's Oedipal gestures of "screwing the earth" and "listening for his father's voice" become expressions of a hopeful future, of a reawakening in the political order of the unity and collectivity conventionally associated with the erotic drive. The erotic relation to history that suffuses the revolutionary culture of the peasants appears first in this

46

Oedipal framework, which is then dilated to represent the symbolic fusion of individual desire and the historical project of the peasantry—a precondition of the utopian transformation of the historical order with which the film concludes.

Alfredo's bourgeois childhood, on the other hand, is associated with a very different aspect of the Oedipal configuration. Here the paternal figure serves as a metaphor of political repression. Intergenerational rivalry is explicitly set out as the breeding ground of the abuse of power that intensifies with each suceeding Padrone. Alfredo's sexuality seems to be entirely informed and conditioned by the contest for power between sons and fathers, which is then projected onto the peasantry.

In the following chapters, I will analyze the ways in which these different perspectives are joined together in the reticule of narrative form. The distinctive use of multiple historical realities illuminated by the psychologies of different characters, and the reciprocal relationship established between public and private orders of events, can be concretely described by analyzing the structure of the film's plot, its character-system, and its narrational techniques, including the use of tense, focalization, and narrative voice.

The Syntax of Plot

1900 begins with the unsettling of the existing political order, setting in motion a chain of narrative actions that can be read either as tending toward the reestablishment of the previous order or toward its permanent overthrow. As Claude Bremond has pointed out, all narratives incline toward the deterioration of an initially stable state or toward the reestablishment of stability in a troubled universe. In *1900*, a certain structural ambiguity is immediately apparent, for the stable state and the troubled universe are one and the same, depending on whether the perspective is from that of the bourgeoisie or the peasantry. What Gerard Genette calls a split narrative focalization—the division of point of view among two or more principal characters—is manifested not only in the control of point of view but also in the formal design of the plot. The narrative method that I will adopt makes this shift in perspective a prominent feature.

The film can be divided into five major sections: the Overture, corresponding to the revolutionary uprising of the peasantry; the Preparatory Section, which takes us back some forty-five years before the events depicted in the Overture and details the childhood of the two principal characters; the Development, or complicating episodes, corresponding to the preFascist years; the Tribulation, or climactic episodes occurring during the Fascist period; and the Denouement, which returns to the temporal frame of the Overture and concludes it, linking together two parts of an interrupted narrative sequence. In addition, an epilogue, or coda, is attached at the end, featuring the two principals as old men.

This structure bears immediate and important consequences for the film's mode of representing history. It imposes an overt teleology upon the historical order, wherein the events of the past will inevitably lead to the present circumstance, with the past seen explicitly as the cause of the present. This teleological aspect gives the viewer prior knowledge of where history will lead. The film thus acknowledges within its own structure the position from the present that informs its reading of the past. Working against this assured and certain outcome, however, is the film's deeper project of showing an alternative end point, its task of rendering events in a manner consistent with its utopian theme. The given order of events calls then for a rereading that will conform both to the empirical order and to the requirements of a visionary history. In this way, the Overture may be seen not simply as the end point of the film's depiction of the historical process, but as the beginning of a new reckoning of historical time. It creates the possibility of a different order of history, or at least a different meaning, emerging from the manifest order of events.

For the most part, however, this secondary figuration of plot events, which would recover the visionary political message the film discovers in the historical order, is not found in the plot design. At the level of the syntax of plot, events are rendered in a "literal" fashion, with the historical order defined strictly in terms of occurrences, actions, and reactions. The secondary or symbolic dimension inhering in the events — the shift in perspective that would cause these events to appear differently, to take on different colors — must be sought in other registers of the narrative structure, particularly the level of tense and the level of the character-system. What the syntax of plot depicts in an overall fashion is that the level of "raw" events favors the Padrone and his class; the historical vision that would empower the peasants is articulated, for the most part, in other registers of the text.

Nevertheless, analysis of the plot design discloses a number of interesting relationships and a very striking pattern regarding the character of Olmo. Plot analysis reveals that Olmo, rather than serving as the Hero in the structure of the tale, functions instead as the Auxiliary, or Donor. The role of Hero is assigned to the entire class of peasants. On the other hand, and contrary to all expectations, the character of Alfredo is not matched against the character Olmo: while Olmo serves the secondary Auxiliary role, Alfredo occupies the cardinal role of Opponent. Alfredo in his capacity as Padrone matches up against the peasant class in a series of polemical encounters. The negative, or false Donor role corresponding to Olmo's positive Donor role is filled by the character of Attila, the Fascist leader. Thus Olmo and Attila are structurally opposed, rather than the anticipated opposition of Olmo and Alfredo. The matching of Olmo and Attila allows another pattern in the text to come into view, which I will here simply characterize as a "salvific" dimension.

In the pages that follow, I will introduce the formal model of plot analysis that I have adopted and detail its workings in a close analysis of the plot syntax of the film. Although at times the model may seem somewhat technical, the value and interest of this approach for *1900* will become evident as the analysis unfolds. I assign a certain priority to plot analysis in this study, for I believe it provides a kind of bedrock of narrative events, transactions, and exchanges, against which the more elusive and abstract elements of narrative design can be measured.

Introduction of the "Move Grammar"

History in *1900* is rendered as a series of polemical encounters. In order to detail its unfolding, I will adopt a model of plot syntax that stresses a problem-resolution format. Labeled "Move Grammar" by Thomas Pavel, this model represents an advance over both the linear system of Vladimir Propp and the achronic systems of Algirdas Greimas and Claude Lévi-Strauss.[1] The method derives not only from these earlier narratological models, but also from Chomskian generative transformational grammar: "The grammar of plot . . . starts from the assumption that narrative structure is a syntactic object, comparable to the syntactic structure of sentences. Thus, Barthes' contention that stories are similar to 'large sentences' is entirely justified" (Pavel 1979, 15).[2] Replacing the category of the sentence in Pavel's narrative grammar is the category of the "Move": "Complex sentences are made up of simple sentences hierarchically linked according to the rules of the grammar. Similarly, the abstract story, which is structured as a complex move, is made up of several simple moves, embedded one under another, according to the prescriptions of the narrative grammar" (1985, 17). This unifying and fundamental category comes from the theory of games: "the main criterion for an action to be considered a *Move* is its impact on the overall strategic situation. An action is a *Move* if it either (directly or indirectly) brings about another *Move*, or if it ends the story" (1985, 15).

Pavel divides the *Move* into two main components, the Problem and the Solution. An intervening function may appear, which contributes to the Solution; it is called the Auxiliary, and corresponds roughly to Propp's Donor or Helper. Two other categories, Circumstance and Tribulation, may also appear between the inauguration of a Problem and its Solution. The method foregrounds the *progressive* logic of narrative unfolding, in that it builds from a completed Solution to a new Problem: the solution of an initial Move, in a conventional narrative, gives rise to a new Problem, whose resolution opens onto a different Problem, and so on. Narrative actions are thus linked together in a directly causal relationship. The Move is "indexed" by the character or "actant" who initiates, performs, or principally benefits from the Move. In a typical plot, two characters will "square off" by commanding alternating Moves, with one character's Solution posing a Problem for the rival character, as in a chess game. Such a structure is called a "polemical configuration."

The Move Grammar devised by Pavel lends itself to an analysis of historical narrative in a particularly felicitous way. Stressing the "logical and causal succession of actions" (Pavel 1985, 34) it corresponds to our intuitive sense of historical consecutiveness. Moreover, it focuses on a question that has been ignored in recent theories of narrative: "what is it that propels narrative forward?" (1985, xix) Applied to the historical narrative, this question bears on historical causation: history and plot may both be triggered by the same form of causation. The primacy accorded the notions of cause and event in this model permits the analysis of the plot of *1900* to serve simultaneously as an analysis of historical representation in the film.

Close Analysis of the Narrative Syntax of *1900:* The Overture

The narrative structure of the Overture of *1900* is particularly interesting, for in a very abridged sequence it sets the major narrative problem, indicates the principal actants and their polemical relationship, and poses as well the ambiguous dual perspective that complicates the film. It can be anatomized as a completed Move and a partial one. As the film opens, a young partisan boy is seen walking in the woods. He is suddenly and unexpectedly machine-gunned to death at point-blank range. As he dies, he utters the statement, "But the war is over!" The murder of the boy constitutes the initial Problem—an act of Villainy (what Propp would label Violation or Lack). The subsequent narrative actions constitute the Solution. Following this initial event, we see two characters. Attila and his wife, desperately trying to escape a band of peasant women, who are in hot pursuit. The two characters are captured and corporally punished—beaten and stabbed with pitchforks. We are encouraged to read this event as Punishment of Villainy.

Although the link between the murder of the boy and the ensuing punishment is very indirect, their syntactic proximity allows us to construe these two narrative actions in a cause and effect relationship. The ambiguity as to whether the bloody capture of Attila constitutes Punishment of Villainy or simply compounds the villainous murder of the boy in the woods in a proliferation of diabolical acts is resolved partially by the logic of the Move structure, by the fact that a complete narrative transaction has taken place in these two events: a Violation that transforms a previously existing state, followed by a response to the Violation that constitutes a Solution. It is also resolved by the fact that the "Patient" or victim of the first attack is a peasant, whose murder is then avenged by other peasants. The Patient of the first action becomes, in effect, the Agent of the second, thus conforming to the alternating Move structure of the "polemical configuration." It can be diagrammed according to Pavel's Move structure in the following fashion:

Move 1

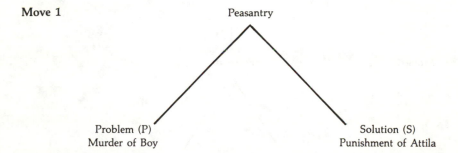

Peasantry

Problem (P)
Murder of Boy

Solution (S)
Punishment of Attila

However, the completed sequence leads to another Problem, for the punishment of Attila by the peasants represents a usurpation of civil authority—he is the Fascist mayor of the town, and has the support not only of the party, but also of the monied classes. This Problem is registered explicitly in the film in the hesitation, the deliberation that follows the taking captive of the Padrone, the traditional and economic authority figure. Hence the initial Solution constitutes a new Problem, which opens onto questions of a historical nature. The peasants are faced with a novel and challenging historical situation, crystallized in the punishment of Attila and the capture of the Padrone: the Problem of the authority and legitimacy of the peasant class. This forms a kind of initial test; their historical role will be decided by the outcome.

The Move, however, can at this point be indexed by both the Padrone and the peasants, for the Padrone is the character who will be principally affected by the Move — he will either be killed or restored to power. The Solution can thus be read dualistically, as either a fall into a Troubled Universe, or as the reestablishment of a previously stable state, depending on who indexes it. The second Move can be charted in the following fashion.

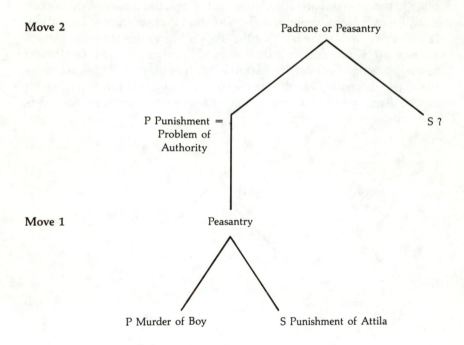

Move 2   Padrone or Peasantry

P Punishment =   S ?
Problem of
Authority

Move 1   Peasantry

P Murder of Boy   S Punishment of Attila

A further refinement of the system of narrative syntax can be offered by observing that all such Solutions can be broken down, subdivided, into a sequence of three stages, each consisting of a choice among alternatives. The narrative system devised by Claude Bremond subdivides any narrative action into three logically necessary processes.[3] These three stages, which eventuate in the Solution, henceforth called Bremond stages, can be diagrammed:

```
                                                             ┌─── successful
                                    ┌─── attempted  - - -     │
              ┌─── considered  - - -│                         └─── unsuccessful
Solution:  ┌──┤                     └─── nonattempted
           │  └─── nonconsidered
```

Plotted according to the Bremond stages, the second Move of the Overture stalls just after the step considered/nonconsidered. The peasant boy who holds the Padrone captive cannot decide whether to preemptorily punish him or whether he should accede to the Padrone's traditional authority. From this perspective the peasant boy is the Agent of the Move, while the Padrone is the Patient. Yet the Move is indexed by both actors, for the outcome affects both of then equally. This same triad of events (Bremond stages) has a "double narrative relevance," (Rimmon-Kenan 1983, 23) and must be indexed redundantly under two character names. Bremond gives the term "joining" to this type of sequence, where what is an improvement in the state of one character will necessarily be a deterioration in the state of another. The abstract Bremond stages can be "filled in" with the concrete content of *1900* and rewritten from these two contrary perspectives in the following fashion, here with the outcome favoring the Padrone (note that this is only a possible narrative outcome, for the Solution to Move 2 is not yet known).

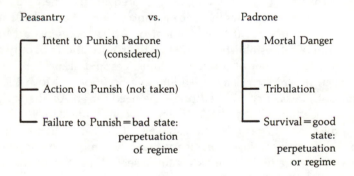

```
Peasantry              vs.          Padrone

┌─── Intent to Punish Padrone       ┌─── Mortal Danger
│        (considered)               │
│                                   │
│                                   │
├─── Action to Punish (not taken)   ├─── Tribulation
│                                   │
│                                   │
└─── Failure to Punish = bad state: └─── Survival = good
        perpetuation                        state:
        of regime                        perpetuation
                                         or regime
```

The Problem, then, is precisely a historical one. Will the peasantry rebel against the ancient feudal system of economic subordination as a further stage of their defiance of the Fascist regime? Will the peasant rebellion grow into a full-fledged revolution? These questions are posed in the narrative in the form of the Problem revolving around the Padrone's authority. Not guilty of murder in the manner of a Fascist thug such as Attila, yet nonetheless connected to the Fascist regime, the Padrone's mutual and contradictory alliances with both the peasantry and the Fascists constitute a quandry that only the process of history can answer. In narratological terms, both the Padrone and the peasantry require an Auxiliary in order to progress to a Solution.

While the seond Move can be indexed variously as the Padrone's or the peasants', it will assume a very different orientation depending on the label we attach to it. Bremond stresses that large-scale, macro-narrative sequences always move in a general direction toward either improvement of a situation or deterioration. Sequences that begin with a Lack or a Violation tend toward reestablishment of an equilibrium; sequences that begin with a steady initial state, on the other hand, will degenerate via the introduction of a Lack or a Problem. Pavel employs the terms Reestablished Universe and Troubled Universe: the Troubled Universe can be "decomposed into an Initial Situation and either a Lack or a Violation. The Reestablished Universe contains a Mediation and a Denouement" (1979, 17).

The narrative events that have unfolded are coded very differently according to the narrative world they affect. In the Padrone's narrative world, the Problem is the Violation of the established order; an initial state, which is more presumed than dramatized at this point, has been disturbed: the Padrone is thus introduced under the sign of a Troubled Universe. For the peasantry, however, the murder of the boy inaugurates the narrative — their plot thus begins with a Violation; moreover, the line of dialogue, "But the war is over!" implies that the peasantry have inhabited a Troubled Universe for some time: the punishment of Attila represents a Move in the direction of a Reestablished Universe, the rectification not only of the murder in Move 1, but of a series of injustices and crimes.

However, the missing element leading to a Solution in Move 2 is identical for both Peasantry and Padrone — the need for an Auxiliary. At this point it is uncertain whether the Auxiliary will contribute to the Reestablishment of the peasant world, which would entail the concomitant degeneration of the Padrone's world, or vice versa. The unique character of the narrative structure of *1900* already can be sensed, for the Auxiliary will simultaneously serve *both* Agents.

A different mapping of the initial functions of the Overture, also utilizing the Bremond stages, can be offered, which allows for the introduction of the Auxiliary function.

The chart below is drawn from the perspective of the peasantry:

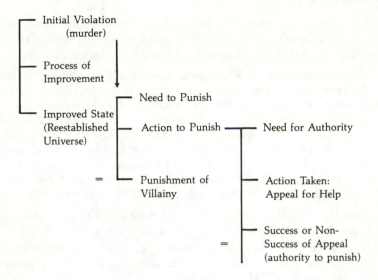

In this analysis, however, we will rely on Pavel's model rather than Bremond's. Bremond's triadic structures, as opposed to Pavel's, are capable of infinite subdivision: each particle of a sequence can be subdivided, and the resulting
subdivisions can be further subdivided, to the point of infinite proliferation. Ultimately, Bremond's system loses both narrative pertinence and a sense of the
dynamic nature of plot, although it can account for the interlocking of narrative structures and the dual perspectivism characteristic of *1900*. Pavel's
model, on the other hand, incorporates the stages model of Bremond in the
definition of the completed Move as the basic, kernel unit of narrative form. But
it concerns itself mainly with those features of narrative that *cause subsequent
events to occur*. Thus a limiting and distinguishing system of pertinences is built
into Pavel's system, where Bremond's is capable of infinite logical subdivision.
By emphasizing events that engender subsequent events, the model conforms to the intuitively progressive nature of narrative unfolding.

The second reason I favor Pavel's model is that it allows the semantic
dimension of the text to be articulated in conjunction with its syntactic
organization. It is evident that to rewrite the Solution of the first Problem —
the punishment of Attila — in terms of the second Problem of legal and
illegal authority requires a reading of the events that is not simply reducible to that of the plot functions. A semantic "fleshing out" of the Problem
is required. Pavel enlists semantic considerations into the snytactic analysis
of plot in two ways. Firstly, the indexing of Moves according to character

names carves out a "narrative domain," or a theater of operations for that character. Secondly, the narrative domain associated with a particular character involves more than simply syntactic relationships:

> Think of the progress of action evaluation and decision-making that takes place every time an actor starts a move. He must discover whether the state of affairs around him is satisfactory, or whether it has to be assessed as constituting a problem. [He must decide] how to react . . . to perform these tasks, a character cannot invent at each step his reasons and way of reacting. Rather, he follows a system of maxims instructing him how to assess the strategic situation and how to react to it . . . As a consequence, the meaning of a given evaluation or decision cannot be fully grasped outside the set of maxims that regulate the judgments and the actions of the characters. (1985, 44–45)

Thus, the context of a narrative event must be taken into consideration in order for its syntactic structure to be comprehensible.[4] In the case of *1900*, and the historical narrative in general, this semantic context is the historical order itself; in Sorlin's words, "common knowledge" guides our reading of the event. This is illustrated in the linking of the murder of the partisan boy and the punishment of Attila. Its meaning becomes clear only through a two-step operation: the indexing of the event under the name of the peasantry, and the invoking of a broader semantic frame — our knowledge of the reference period, which allows us to interpret the events in the manner I have described. Here the historical narrative differs from other narrative works, for the set of maxims governing character actions can, at least initially, be discerned according to our knowledge of the reference period. The syntactic-semantic analysis of the Overture reveals that the main problem revolves around the class issue of the peasantry versus the bourgeoisie. The global Problem of the film's narrative structure is adumbrated in the issue of authority posed in Move 2 of the Overture.

The Second Movement: The Preparatory Section

The second movement of the narrative, which reverts to a historical period forty-five years prior to the events depicted in the Overture, can be considered an Initial Situation or Preparatory Section. The inaugural exposition of situation, place, and character is thus displaced in *1900*, deferred until after the first set of narrative Moves rendered in the Overture. The Preparatory Section is introduced prior to the completion of the Moves begun in the Overture, interrupting the Overture *in medias res*. It is as if the Solution to the Problem of authority can only be resolved by reverting to the past, as if to seek the key to the present disorder in the lessons of the past. This second section of the film manifests the general quality of a stable universe, with no major violations. Here the situation is established and the *dramatis personae* introduced. The segment cannot be labeled either as a deteriorating sequence or as an improving one. Nonetheless, it unfolds according to the narrative logic and sequencing I have outlined above. Even the simplest narrative episodes, those that appear to be merely anecdotal or descriptive, operate according to a problem-solving logic.

The initial scene of the Preparatory Section begins with a shot of a figure dressed in motley, staggering drunkenly down a road, lamenting that "Verdi is dead!" At one level, the scene marks the temporal frame of the film — the end of the nineteenth century — and indicates that the narrative begins at a point of transition. At another level, however, that of structure, this scene opens the film under the sign of a Lack. Verdi's death is represented as a loss, as a sudden dispossession; it can be read symbolically as the destabilization of an established way of life. The syntagmatic thrust of the Preparatory Section, its initiating Problem, is thus set in motion by the force of a historical event, an event that invokes the historical order. History is seen as the accelerator of the opening Move of the main body of the narrative.

The ensuing narrative event is introduced in such a way as to represent a Solution. To the Problem of the destabilization of the mode of life of the nineteenth century, the film presents a Solution in the form of the dual births of the characters Olmo and Alfredo. These two events — the death of Verdi and the double births — are linked syntactically, but in a way that suggests a symbolic and not a causal connection. What can be described as a perturbation in the historical order is here resolved by the birth of two children who will represent their respective classes into the twentieth century. Hence the first two scenes of the Preparatory Section can be diagrammed as such:

Move 1

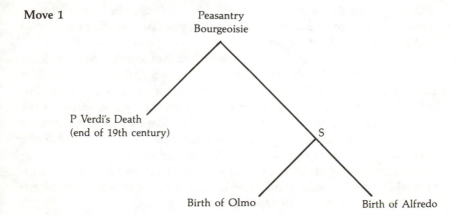

57

The syntactic linkage of these two narrative events forges an immediate bond between the historical order and the personal plot line of the individual characters. The syntactic couplet of Problem and Solution fuses two events that occur at very different semantic levels. This syntactic bridging of different semantic orders occurs frequently in the film, giving it a strongly allegorical quality: events occurring at the personal, individual level are figuratively linked to the larger historical order. Nevertheless, a clear-cut narrative logic and momentum, an almost clockwork narrative progression from Problem to Solution, governs the transit from the personal to the historical. A kind of forward-progress momentum is thus maintained, in spite of the dramatic shifts in semantic level that characterize the film.

The initial Solution, involving the two births into the opposing classes, can be represented with consistency in the model we are employing. But the dual assignment of the Move function, with both the peasantry and the bourgeoisie sharing the initial Move, cannot be accommodated in this model, founded as it is on a pattern of polemical confrontation. The Bremond feature of *joining* narratives described above, with its possibility of dual assignment of the protagonist of the Move, is really not compatible with Pavel's model, with its insistent pattern, derived from game-theory, of alternating Moves. Thus we must decide who underwrites the first Move of the Preparatory Section. Put another way, we must sharpen the question of who benefits from the Solution. For a variety of reasons, the first narrative Move will prove to favor the bourgeoisie.

The birth of Alfredo perpetuates the bourgeois line into the twentieth century, and hence constitutes a Solution for a Move indexed by the bourgeoisie. But this Solution also encompasses the birth of Olmo, son of the peasant class, in that the dual births promise to perpetuate the class relations of the nineteenth century into the twentieth. The little bourgeois comes into the world equipped with a little peasant, ensuring the continued existence of the bourgeois class.

What is a Solution for the bourgeoisie, however, constitutes a Problem for the peasantry. Rather than an heir, Olmo is a bastard; rather than a positive extension of the family, ensuring its survival, he is seen as another mouth to feed, stretching and weakening the thin resources of the clan. A kind of doubled symmetry operates here in the opening Move structure. The Solution for one class encompasses *both* births, while the Problem for the other class is identically configured: the birth of the peasant Olmo and that of Alfredo comprise the initial Problem for the peasantry, which can be understood in wider terms as the continuation of oppression into the twentieth century.

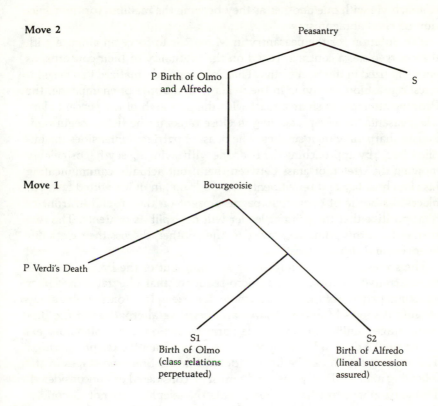

Move 2   Peasantry

P Birth of Olmo
and Alfredo   S

Move 1   Bourgeoisie

P Verdi's Death

S1
Birth of Olmo
(class relations
perpetuated)

S2
Birth of Alfredo
(lineal succession
assured)

Note that we have established from the outset a very neat polemical configuration. The twin births are immediately deployed into a Problem structure, which dramatizes the antagonistic relation between the classes. The Marxian *topos* of antagonistic classes here stands in for what could easily be described as a mythic *topos* of enemy brothers, with the theme of the twin births serving as the vehicle for a history of the classes — a kind of Romulus and Remus legend updated for the founding of a new civilization (see Horton 1980, 12). Thus we see that the narrative momentum is already very strong. Polemical configurations are cast up in seemingly natural fashion by the kernel narrative device of doubled characters who are born into an adversarial relationship. Here the two children do not so much vie with one another as they become the medium for the depiction of class antagonism.

The Solution for the peasantry in Move 2 is to forge an alliance with the bourgeoisie, a contract, based on the mutuality of their concerns, as emblematized in the twin births. This Solution is dramatized in a very interesting fashion. Arriving in the fields with a bottle of champagne, the Padrone attempts to share a toast with the patriarch of the peasant clan. The peasants, however, standing in close ranks in the fields, begin ominously sharpening their scythes. The peasant patriarch intensifies the implied threat by approaching the Padrone with swinging scythe, ostensibly mowing the stretch of grass between them, but actually communicating his class hostility and resentment. The Padrone, in quick-witted fashion, places the bottle of open champagne upright on the ground in front of him, positive that the peasant leader will not spill its contents. The two patriarchs at this point acknowledge one another, discuss their class differences, and drink a toast.

The scene provides an interesting working out of the Bremond stages to a narrative Solution. It is a micro-sequence that illustrates the larger structural patterns of the text as a whole. It is exemplary for narrative study because it shows both the positive and negative alternatives of the Bremond stages, unlike a more simple narrative action. An explanatory example can be drawn. James Bond is in a room when the telephone rings. The ensuing action can be broken down into its Bremond stages in the following manner. Firstly, the action must be considered or nonconsidered. This corresponds to whether Bond hears the telephone or not. Secondly, if he hears it, he must *decide* whether to attempt action — to answer the phone — or not. Thirdly, the action, if taken, will either be successful or unsuccessful: for example, he might be distracted en route to the telephone, or be ambushed in his transit across the room; he might already be wounded, bound and gagged, and/or unable to speak — in other words, he may not be able to physically complete the action once commenced. In most narratives, however, this sequence, with all of its implicit narrative potential, will be collapsed into the simple and direct action of picking up the phone and speaking into it. The second Move of the Preparatory Section, the incident centered on the bottle of champagne, displays the more protracted narrative realization I have just described. Here the solution — ultimately, the killing of the Padrone — is both considered and not yet fully considered: it is merely intimated in the collective sharpening of the peasants' blades. Secondly, something like symbolic action is taken, but the actual commission of battery is not. Thirdly, the gesture is both successful and not completely successful. The alliance has the effect of pacifying both parties, but the essential class inequities are still preserved. This sequence, with its simultaneous staging of actions and their possible alternatives, provides the model for the major configurations of the plot.

The Solution to the Problem can be described as a new alliance between the peasantry and the bourgeoisie, one founded on the recognition of the stability of the existing class structure. A problem in narrative indexing arises here, however, for it would seem that the Move could be commanded equally by the Padrone, who has staved off violence by his quick action, or by the peasantry, who have here renewed a more or less benevolent relationship. The episode might therefore be perceived from the Padrone's point of view, with the action taken serving as a Solution to a threat. To preserve the alternating, adversarial format of one Move squaring off against another, it is necessary to inscribe the Move from the peasants' point of view. We must thus invoke, once again, a semantic component to guide our reading. This will involve a reference to the historical situation in which the characters find themselves. With this in mind, it is evident that the alliance favors the peasantry and, in fact, an alliance is the best the peasants can manage. At this point, history itself places the peasants at a disadvantage. We will find that the Moves commanded by the peasants always have something equivocal or partial about them. They are not definitive Solutions, at least until the point of the general strike. The Moves commanded by the bourgeoisie, on the other hand, are complete, emphatic, and even overplayed, with multiple Solutions to a single Problem tipping the balance of the polemical configuration.

According to this reading of the second Move, which I have indexed as the peasants' Solution, the bottle of champagne becomes the key element, not the Padrone's quick wits. The bottle of wine serves as the Auxiliary, aiding in the Solution, providing the necessary mediation. Something like a shared code or an existential link, it represents a contract or treaty between the two classes that will continue while both patriarchs still live. The alliance lends a quality of prelapsarian plenitude to the early childhood of both heirs.

In the ensuing section, the film lingers on a number of scenic details. In what is really a long descriptive passage, the separate class identities of Olmo and Alfredo are established; but the alliance between the two classes is also stressed through the childhood friendship of the two boys. They each have access to the other's domain; they appear to share the same girlfriend; they engage in a series of equalizing challenges and tests, in which Olmo generally emerges the victor. Nevertheless, their inherited class identities are stamped upon them. I will describe a typical scene from this movement of the narrative. Although the scene is highly significant on the thematic and symbolic level, it cannot be entered into our narrative "tree," for it does not affect additional Moves or augment the significant narrative action in any way. It expresses quite well, however, the general tone of the Preparatory Section of the narrative, and is interesting in its own right, for it adheres to the Problem-Solution format outlined above.

The scene can be described as a rite of passage for the two boys, a passage into full-fledged membership in their respective classes. It involves a kind of trial, or test, of alimentary fortitude. The enterprising Olmo has established a commercial relationship with the cook at the villa, whom he supplies with frogs. One evening, the child Alfredo discovers that his dinner consists of nothing other than Olmo's catch of the day. He becomes sick and refuses to eat, causing his father to punish him. His father in turn is punished by the grand old patriarch, as we are treated to the comic sight of three generations of Padrones simultaneously booting each other in the rear. Meanwhile, in a parallel scene, Olmo is called to task by the patriarch of the peasant clan for not sharing the gold piece he received for the frogs. He is placed on top of the table, and symbolically initiated into the clan by the recital of its collective code. He has no father, therefore he belongs to all of the group. Conversely, he must place the needs of the group in the forefront: what is his becomes the clan's. This said, food and wine are given to Olmo, and the gold piece is surrendered.

Now a thematic reading of these two parallel episodes bears interesting results. The events around the table constitute a symbolic initiation into class identity. The hostility at the bourgeois table is expressive of an alimentary code of exclusion: to eat food that is coded as the raw, as a species of nature, (not literally raw, but in the sense in which Lévi-Strauss uses the term), is paradoxically to enter the privileged class. For Alfredo, the food here represents a Problem, illustrating a certain weakening of his class identity. For Olmo, on the other hand, the food serves as the emblem of communality and inclusiveness.[5] Fed with stew and wine, he is marked as belonging to a culture of peasants; he is subsumed into a larger chain, which has a positive alimentary coding, and which for him represents a Solution. The film is consistent, even in these minor, subordinate narrative episodes, in presenting a very clear-cut Problem-Solution structure. The conflict here is intramural, however, rather than between the classes, and thus cannot be represented in the narrative tree I have devised. The strong structure I have distinguished in the text is the polemical configuration, and it is the class rivalry, rather than conflict within the class, that generates further plot events.

The deaths of the two patriarchs constitutes the next major narrative event from the point of view of the functional syntax. The event is coded as a Problem, for the charismatic alliance of the peasantry and the bourgeoisie is hereby destroyed. The two deaths mark the fall into a Troubled Universe, for the farm cannot sustain itself under the regime of the second Padrone, and the peasant class no longer has a leader: there is no one to forge a new bond with the second Padrone, who is in every way villainous, a characteristic clearly indicated by his fraudulent altering of the terms of his inheritance.

True to the polemical configuration that has developed between the two classes, the next Move is indexed by the second Padrone. His Solution to the Problem of the breakup of the alliance is to exploit the peasantry. He begins to mechanize the farm and cuts the workers' share in half. Thus we have a narrative tree that now looks like this:

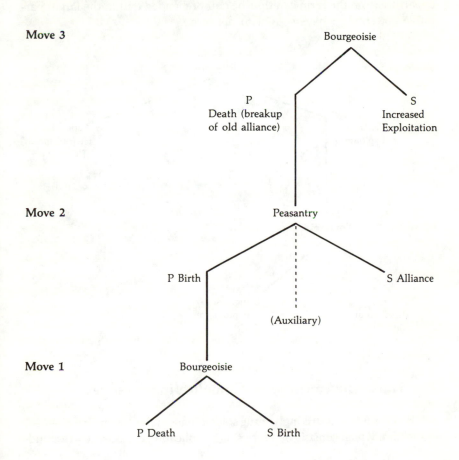

Move 3

Bourgeoisie

P
Death (breakup
of old alliance)

S
Increased
Exploitation

Move 2

Peasantry

P Birth

S Alliance

(Auxiliary)

Move 1

Bourgeoisie

P Death

S Birth

The subsequent Problem for the peasantry is obviously this selfsame exploitation that constitutes a Solution in Move 3. But the situation in Move 4 is complicated by the absence of a leader for the peasant class. The Solution, as in Move 2, requires an Auxiliary. Thus the first two Moves indexed by the peasantry require the help of an Auxiliary. Moreover, the Solution here is precisely the Appeal for Help. Ultimately, a general strike will be called against the landowning class, representing a Solution that takes nearly a decade to accomplish. At this point, however, the absence of a peasant leader eliminates the possibility of such an action. The Appeal for Help in Move 4 takes the form of the Proppian function of Dispatch. Olmo is sent off to school, away from the estate; when he returns he will assume the role of class leader. He will be defined in this role only until his larger narrative function of Auxiliary or Donor is disclosed. Olmo's departure from the farm can thus be comprehended within the larger narrative patterning I have sought to disclose.

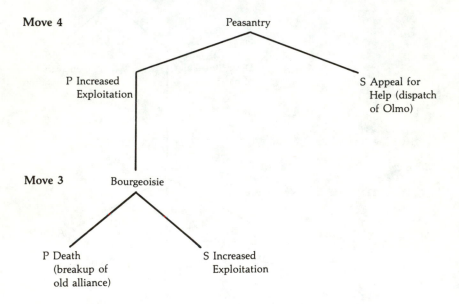

The Third Movement: The Complicating Episodes

Olmo's return as a strikingly virile soldier inaugurates the third movement of the film, which consists of a series of complicating episodes, corresponding to the preFascist years. The return, which completes the Solution of Move 4 on behalf of the peasantry, can be read as a Problem for the second Padrone. The text makes this evident. It highlights Olmo's return as both a Solution for the peasantry and a Problem for the Padrone by installing an Opponent at the villa in order to balance the advantage gained for the peasantry by Olmo's return. The new foreman, Attila, is introduced simultaneously with Olmo's arrival at the farm. He is immediately cast in an adversarial role. His brute strength, his sadism in enforcing the quota system, his outsized villainy — are all immediately emphasized and form a striking contrast to Olmo's radiant masculine virtue. Attila can be seen as the answer to an implied Appeal for Help indexed by the Padrone, symmetrical to the earlier Move by the peasants. He represents the Padrone's Solution in Move 5. I will thus map the arrival of Attila as a function *caused* by Olmo's return, although this will create an anachronism in our structure, as the text clearly places Attila at the farm prior to Olmo's arrival. We will nevertheless preserve the linear logic of the narrative if we situate the arrival of Attila in a posterior position in our narrative tree, despite the fact that we will hereby violate the surface chronology of the diegesis.

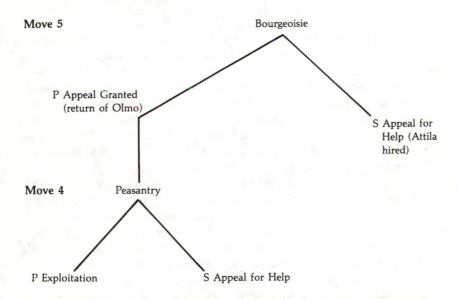

Move 5   Bourgeoisie

P Appeal Granted
(return of Olmo)

                                                  S Appeal for
                                                  Help (Attila
                                                  hired)

Move 4   Peasantry

P Exploitation   S Appeal for Help

The victimization of the peasantry intensifies with Attila's cruelty and the Padrone's continued exploitation. The peasants' next Solution is a

The character of Alfredo, the scion of the ruling class, is a purely virtual character, holding the position of the future Padrone as a kind of open potentiality. The new equilibrium between the classes is expressed in the revival of the friendship of Olmo and Alfredo. They travel to town together, attempt to share the same girl, and seem to exist harmoniously, despite their manifest class differences. (1990 Copyright © 1976 PEA Produzioni Europee Associate-Rome. All Rights Reserved. Courtesy of Paramount Pictures.)

general strike. It is a successful Solution and reestablishes a certain equilibrium between the classes. I will index the Move as Olmo's, even though it is his wife who is the true revolutionary leader. Olmo's wife, Anita, may be understood as an Auxiliary, in spite of her leadership role in the strike. Although the role of Anita is highly significant at the symbolic and the thematic levels, her structural position remains that of the Auxiliary—essentially, preparing Olmo in his leadership role. Her quick disappearance from the universe of the film after this Move is completed confirms this designation. Again, we find that the Moves commanded by the peasantry are characterized by their use of the Auxiliary.

The character of Alfredo, the scion of the ruling class, has been undeveloped in the narrative up until this point. He is a purely virtual character, nascent, holding the position of the future Padrone as a kind of open potentiality. Nothing he has done so far has had an impact on the plot. The new equilibrium between the classes is expressed, however, in the revival of the friendship of Olmo and Alfredo. They travel to town together, attempt to share the same girl, and seem to exist harmoniously, despite their manifest class differences. Meanwhile, Olmo's wife educates the peasantry in a small school near the villa. These sequences, however, representing a kind of temporary peace, are descriptive, rather than narratively important, and thus cannot be worked into the narrative tree above.

Of far greater consequence narratively is the response of Alfredo's father, the second Padrone, to the general strike. The Problem caused by the increased power of the peasantry eventuates in the Padrone organizing the landowners into a committee that will ally itself with the new Fascist party. The Solution to the Problem of the increased power of the peasants involves Attila. Thus a neat symmetrical structure unfolds: to Olmo's new political leadership, augmented by the revolutionary teachings of his wife, the Padrone counters with an Opponent, Attila, who is installed as the head of the local Fascist chapter.

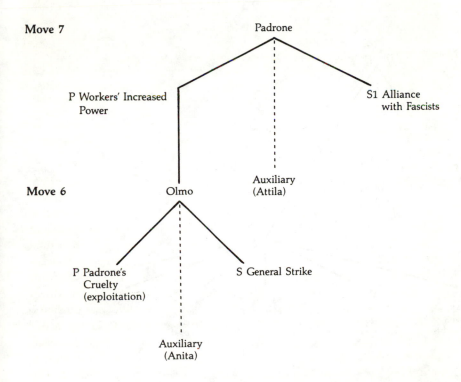

Move 7

Padrone

P Workers' Increased Power

S1 Alliance with Fascists

Auxiliary (Attila)

Move 6 Olmo

P Padrone's Cruelty (exploitation)

S General Strike

Auxiliary (Anita)

The Padrone's Solution to the newfound power of the workers following the strike is the alliance with the Fascists. Narratively, this Move is subdivided into a number of local, punctual solutions, spread over a number of years, all of which stem from the original alliance with the Fascists. These serial Solutions, which are implied by the alliance and flow from it—and thus will be grouped beneath it—commence with the torching of the school where Anita teaches. Three peasant elders who were inside the building are immolated. The Solutions continue to be imposed in a similar manner, as we witness a catalogue of Fascist crimes, consisting of the sexual assault and murder of a young boy, the false indictment of Olmo, the general persecution of the peasantry along with the more unfortunate members of the old aristocracy, and finally the mass murder of the peasants. This part of the narrative consists of the years of Fascist terror, and marks the end of the period of tranquillity following the general strike. The long Tribulation of the peasants is underway. Accordingly, we find a slightly different narrative configuration:

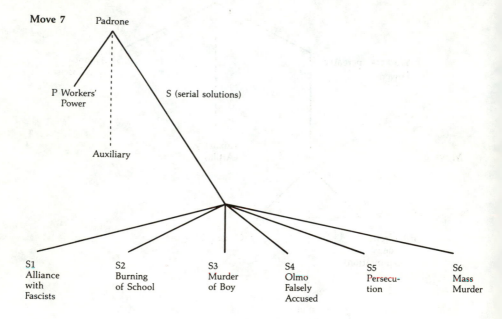

The Fourth Movement: The Tribulation

The death of the second Padrone is the event that marks Move 8. Although the peasants do not cause the death, they stand to benefit from it: hence the Move will be indexed by the peasantry. Now for the first time the Move structure diverges significantly from the chronological order of the plot. The death of the second Padrone and Alfredo's assumption of power occur temporally just prior to the murder of the young boy, represented as Solution 3 to Move 7. All of the subsequent Solutions to Move 7 occur well *after* the event we are labeling Move 8. What the chart indicates as occurring *after* the sequence of violent Solutions actually occurs in the midst of them. Logically, however, this order is consistent, for the whole sequence of Solutions derives clearly from the original alliance with the Fascists, which continues over a number of years and which extends across the regime of the second Padrone and into the regime of Alfredo. The fact that certain Solutions are *already in place* prior to Alfredo's assumption of power — Solutions that occur during his regime but that *logically* predate his arrival at the position of power — indicate something of the weakness of the character. Alfredo will command only unsuccessful Moves. He is at every piont upstaged by Attila in providing the Solutions, which are, as we have seen in our chart, already laid out. The original conflictual dynamic between peasantry and bourgeoisie is to some degree skewed by the ascendance of Attila, who begins to attain greater autonomy and power as the film progresses. Nevertheless, at this point, the Move structure maintains the position of the Padrone as the nominal indexer of the Moves.

The first Problem Alfredo faces as Padrone presents him with mutually antagonistic Solutions. His initial narrative act as the new Padrone is designed to correct two Lacks: the lack of an heir and the lack of power. He commands the next Move in the form of an assertive act — marriage — meant to correct the first Lack. But the marriage ceremony also serves as the occasion for Alfredo to attempt to correct the second Lack — the lack of power — through the further enfranchisement of Attila. These are unsuccessful Solutions: in fact, they are mutually exclusive, as we shall see shortly.

While Alfredo here begins to index Moves for the first time, a manifest but curiously disengaged struggle seems to be developing between Attila and Olmo, which we might label the "Battle of the Auxiliaries." Yet the actions commanded by Olmo do not deal with Attila in a direct way. The confrontations between Olmo and Attila are marked by Olmo's restraint. Twice he nearly takes action against Attila: in terms of the Bremond stages, he has twice considered and twice rejected direct action against his Opponent. As we shall see, this is only an apparent polemical configuration. Olmo cannot engage directly with Attila, for his true role is not that of the Hero, but that of the Donor or Auxiliary. It is noteworthy that in Greimas's six-part table of actantial roles, consisting of the logical pairs Subject/Object, Sender/Receiver, Auxiliary/Opponent, the Auxiliary and

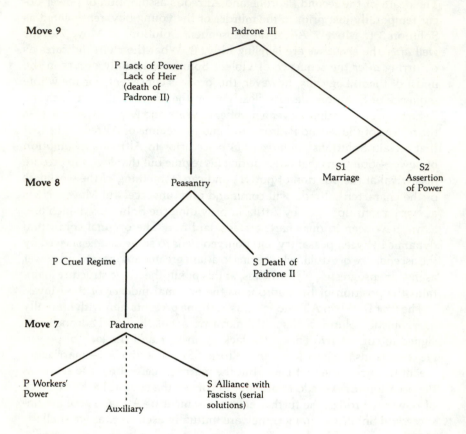

Move 9   Padrone III

                        P Lack of Power
                        Lack of Heir
                        (death of
                        Padrone II)

                                                              S1   S2
                                                              Marriage   Assertion
                                                                              of Power
Move 8   Peasantry

              P Cruel Regime   S Death of
                                                      Padrone II

Move 7   Padrone

P Workers'   S Alliance with
Power   Fascists (serial
                        Auxiliary   solutions)

the Opponent oppose one another, rather than the more conventional Prop-pian model of Subject (Hero)/(Villain).[6] It would seem that Greimas's system fits the present case. Neither character squares off against the other, but each assists in the Moves commanded by their separate "houses" or "moieties." The original polemical configuration between bourgeois and peasant is thus maintained in spite of the textual prominence of the Fascist Attila, precisely because Attila and Olmo are relegated to *indirect combat,* as befits Auxiliaries. Were they to square off directly, the Move structure would reflect something other than the clear-cut class polarities that we have seen so far. Attila, after all, comes from the lower classes as well. The reasons for keeping Olmo at the level of the Auxiliary may perhaps

Alfredo's marriage to Ada and his enfranchisement of Attila, affirming his importance as the Padrone's "watchdog," are meant as dual solutions to two Lacks: lack of an heir and lack of power. But the two solutions are mutually exclusive. Ada is revolted by Attila and his Blackshirt friends, and Alfredo's secret empowerment of Attila is guaranteed to drive Ada away. (1990 Copyright © 1976 PEA Produzioni Europee Associate-Rome. All Rights Reserved. Courtesy of Paramount Pictures.)

be found in the Marxian theme of the film, with its collective rather than individual notion of the Hero. For the purposes of narrative description, however, the very curious absence of direct engagement between Olmo and Attila underlines their clear-cut parallel function as Auxiliaries.

At this point in the central narrative tree, the Moves associated with the position of the Padrone, which were so decisive and emphatic in the early part of the narrative, begin to work against his own self-interest. Alfredo's marriage to Ada and his enfranchisement of Attila, affirming his importance as the Padrone's "watchdog," are meant as dual solutions to two Lacks: lack of an heir and lack of power. But the two Solutions to Move 9 are mutually exclusive, and cause a new Problem for Alfredo that will not be resolved in the course of the film. Ada is revolted by Attila and his Blackshirt friends, and Alfredo's secret empowerment of Attila — who wanted to leave the estate — is guaranteed to drive Ada away.

This point is driven home in the scenes immediately following Attila's interview with Alfredo. Newly charged with providing "security" for the

Ada expresses her rage and despair at Alfredo's lack of action as the Fascists beat Olmo severely. Alfredo's desire for power, which involves a corrupt bargain with the Fascists, and his desire for his wife cannot both be sustained. The contradictory impulses of Alfredo — inclined both to liberalism and to Fascism, friend of Olmo and sponsor of Attila — have immediate consequences now that Alfredo is the Padrone. (1990 Copyright © 1976 PEA Produzioni Europee Associate-Rome. All Rights Reserved. Courtesy of Paramount Pictures.)

estate, Attila and his consort Regina repair to an isolated shed on the grounds to have sex. They discover that they are being watched by a young boy who had been attracted to Attila's black leather gloves. They force the boy to participate, after which Attila murders him. In a parallel scene, cross-cut with the sex scene, Ada is seen riding a white charger, "Cocaine," given to her as a wedding present. She comes upon Olmo walking in the fields, and they converse. As Ada and Olmo approach the scene of the crime, the body is discovered. Attila promptly accuses Olmo of the crime, and he and his Fascist henchmen begin beating Olmo severely. The Padrone, knowing Olmo is innocent via the direct testimony of his wife, to say nothing of his certain knowledge of Olmo's moral character, stands by as the Fascists beat Olmo. Ada expresses her rage and despair at Alfredo's lack of action: the two Solutions that the wedding promised to produce have already begun to cancel one another out; the two Solutions have themselves become a Problem. Alfredo's desire for power, which involves a corrupt bargain with the Fascists, and his desire for his wife cannot both be sustained. The contradictory impulses of Alfredo — inclined to both liberalism and Fascism, friend of Olmo and sponsor of Attila — have immediate consequences that are incapable of resolution in the course of the narrative, now that Alfredo is the Padrone.

The assertion of power by Alfredo has both direct and long-term consequences for the peasantry. In the most immediate sense, the Problem for the peasantry is the direct effect of Alfredo's assertion of power, namely, the beating of Olmo. This Problem constitutes the next Move indexed by the peasantry. It is solved in a fashion that is typical of the Moves commanded by the peasantry, for it involves an Auxiliary. Let us return to the beating of Olmo. As the corporal punishment administered to Olmo intensifies, a man, a kind of gypsy wanderer, enters the scene, claiming that it was he, not Olmo, who committed the crime. The man is seized and carried off to the authorities, as the punishment of Olmo finally ceases. Here a Helper has come along to rescue Olmo by volunteering himself as a scapegoat. In a sense, this function of scapegoat is served by both Olmo and by the wanderer. Olmo has in fact been made the scapegoat for the Padrone's combination of sexual jealousy and insecurity regarding his power. The wanderer, on the other hand, in becoming the scapegoat for Olmo, fulfills the role of Auxiliary, which Olmo cannot fulfill at this point. The wanderer performs Olmo's role by proxy, thus retaining the matching structure of Auxiliaries working on behalf of their respective classes. This event can be represented in the following fashion:

Move 10

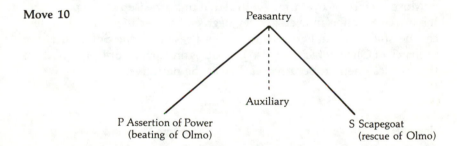

Peasantry

Auxiliary

P Assertion of Power
(beating of Olmo)

S Scapegoat
(rescue of Olmo)

On the part of the Padrone, the problem created by the two incompatible Solutions in Move 9 continues to perplex his narrative world. He is offered a choice several times by Ada: marriage and children or the power he commands through Attila. Unable to decide, Alfredo first loses Ada and then decides to repudiate Attila. There is no affirmative Solution to Move 11. Instead, we see a rapid degeneration of the Padrone's universe because of his inability to act. The Solution here can only be designated negatively: it consists of the loss of Ada and the loss of power, for Attila rather than Alfredo is now in a position of authority. He is the Fascist mayor of the town and acts on his own volition: the Padrone wrests no power from Attila by finally repudiating him.

Move 11

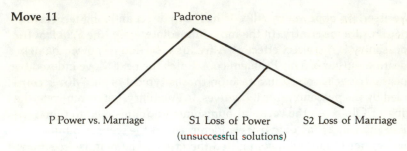

P Power vs. Marriage   S1 Loss of Power   S2 Loss of Marriage
(unsuccessful solutions)

Thus Alfredo, as Padrone, commands only one affirmative Move, which is the marriage and the assertion of power, and even that Move backfires. He has created a Problem for himself with this one Move that haunts him until the close of the narrative. In many ways, Alfredo's role has been played out by this point in the film, as he commands no further actions that advance the plot.

But the loss of power Alfredo suffers has a manifest impact, once more, on the peasantry. As Attila has grown in power, the situation deteriorates still further. The Tribulation of the peasantry, which I have represented in Move 7, worsens over time; with Attila unleashed upon the populace, the peasants suffer an even greater degree of persecution. The Problem can be stated as the Persecution of the Peasantry: the Solution is the Dispatch of Olmo, which can also be read as an Appeal for Help — a Move that echoes one that occurred earlier in the narrative.

Move 12

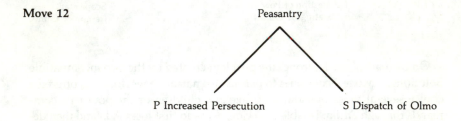

P Increased Persecution   S Dispatch of Olmo

The dispatch of Olmo is somewhat disguised in the plot, given a diegetic alibi, by an incident that the film stages seemingly for the express purpose of causing Olmo to leave. That incident occurs when Olmo insults and humiliates Attila by pelting him with horse manure. This forces Olmo to escape from the estate or Attila will surely have him killed. Nonetheless, the deeper plot function of Dispatch or Appeal for Help is fulfilled by the event of Olmo's flight, a Move consistent with the pattern of Moves commanded by the peasantry. Thus what looks like a simple escape, from the point of view of the diegesis, is in fact an assertive Move by the peasantry that will ultimately fulfill the requirement that the peasants employ an Auxiliary in their battle with the Fascists, which at this point has displaced the battle with the bourgeoisie.

The escape of Olmo is clearly coded as a Problem for Attila, who wreaks his predictable vengeance on the populace at large, eventuating in the mass murder of the peasants. This retribution by Attila was rendered earlier as a variant to the Solution in Move 7, where it was indexed by the Padrone, with Attila as Auxiliary. Here it is Attila, or the Fascists, who index the Move. I will label Attila's revenge, the mass murder of the peasants, as the Solution to Move 13, because it represents Attila's "graduation" from Auxiliary to indexer of the Move. The event can be represented in the following fashion:

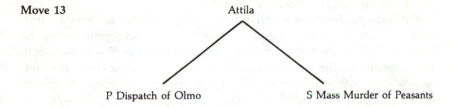

Move 13   Attila

P Dispatch of Olmo   S Mass Murder of Peasants

This incident brings to a close the Tribulation of the peasant class, marking the end of the sustained fourth movement of the film. The murders that begin and end this movement—the sex murder of the boy and the mass murder of the peasants—are logically linked as aspects of the Solution initiated by the second Padrone, continued and consolidated by Alfredo, and carried out by Attila. The Tribulation is, in effect, the working out over time of the consequences of the Padrones' alliance with the Fascists. By the end of this section, the consequences of this alliance are clear: the character of Attila has replaced the character of the Padrone in the Move structure, who is in effect "bracketed" in terms of his effectivity in the plot. Although this mainly indicates the loss of the Padrone's power and the growth of Attila's, it also preserves a certain symmetry in the roles played by Alfredo and Olmo. While Alfredo is figuratively absent, Olmo is literally absent from this segment of the narrative design.

The Fifth Movement: The Denouement

The first Move of the Denouement, the final section of the film, brings us back to the scenes that opened the film, thus closing the temporal loop opened by the initial flashback and allowing us to join the detached Moves of the Overture to the rest of the narrative tree. We recall that the opening scene of the film immediately presents the viewer with a murder. The murder of the partisan boy in the woods, we surmised, was probably the indirect reason behind the pursuit and punishment of Attila. Now, the agency behind the murder can be established directly: the murder constitutes the last in a series of Fascist Solutions, the last in a series of peasant Tribulations. Rather than seeming unmotivated, accidental, occurring after the war is already over, the murder now appears to be motivated by the whole course of cause and effect linkages that have occurred throughout the narrative. The punishment of Attila is now presented again, but this time as an inevitable consequence of events — the seemingly arbitrary relationship between the murder of the boy and the punishment of Attila is clarified, as the peasants pursue Attila in a Move that is an exact rehearsal of the opening moments of the film.

While the punishment of Attila, which is the Solution to Move 14, proceeds with swift dispatch, the problem of authority revolving around the issue of the Padrone has yet to be resolved. It is this problem, we recall, that necessitated the long analepsis that comprised the body of the film, an analepsis that seemed to marshal the "evidence of history" in order to arrive at a justifiable Solution.

The return of Olmo in the role of Auxiliary facilitates the Solution. What is most interesting is that Olmo's return serves *both* sides of the polemical relationship. The lack of authority to punish — the problem of what to do with the Padrone — will be resolved in exactly the manner of a previous narrative resolution: the formation of a new alliance. Alfredo is to be spared, but the Padrone's power will be abolished. The last Move of the film, then, can ultimately be indexed by both the Padrone and by the peasantry; they could be said to "share" the Move, for both sides benefit by the Solution. Alfredo survives, in the face of almost certain execution, while the peasants, for their part, gain a measure of authority and freedom. Olmo's role as Auxiliary has in effect been transformed into that of mediator: an Auxiliary for both sides.

Rather than seeing this as an equivocation in the narrative structure, I see it as a way of keeping the narrative structure relatively open. The forging of the new alliance has something temporary and provisional about it; the implication is that additional narrative "leaves" could be grafted onto

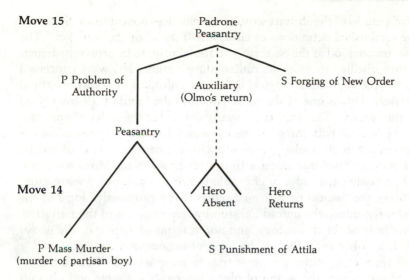

Move 15

Padrone
Peasantry

P Problem of
Authority

Auxiliary
(Olmo's return)

S Forging of New Order

Peasantry

Move 14

Hero
Absent

Hero
Returns

P Mass Murder
(murder of partisan boy)

S Punishment of Attila

the tree, that history is ongoing, and that the narrative closure that results from this "sharing" of the narrative Move is only a kind of formal finish to the design — the consummation of a pattern, rather than a definitive, determinative ending.

Reflections on the Model

The fact that Move 14 repeats the opening Move of the film from the Overture crystallizes the larger problem of the relation between chronological order, order of presentation, and Move structure that has been raised earlier. Pavel goes to some length to present a rationale for the priority of the Move structure in analyzing plot:

> All proposed varieties of narrative structures, our trees included, have at least an abstract narrative level, in which the order of ultimate constituents (events) can be different from the chronological order . . . Indeed, from a chronological point-of-view, the Moves are not compact entities. The Solution to a Problem can arrive long after its first appearance. Chronological order is thus a property of individual events rather than entire Moves. As a consequence, it cannot be located at a very abstract level of plot structure . . . A more abstract analysis shows the relative independence of the logical narrative structure from the chronological order of events (1985, 34).

Pavel's model of the abstract structure of plot does not conform, therefore, to the established definitions of either the "fabula" or the "syuzhet." The fabula, understood as the basic story material prior to its artistic ordering, the story distilled to its basic, rudimentary outline, is always conceived in terms of straight chronological order: the unfolding of events in natural succession. This is one of the principal ways the fabula is distinguished from the syuzhet. The syuzhet is usually defined as the order of presentation, the "artistic patterning" of events, which frequently presents the occurrences out of chronology, depending on the particular kind of artistic effect sought. Pavel introduces a third coordinate in his Move structure, which is neither the order of chronology nor the order of presentation, but rather the "logical narrative structure." The progressive logic of the model foregrounds the unfolding, step-by-step progress of the narrative, but not in terms of chronology, and not in terms of artistic or discursive form, but rather according to the logic of actions and agency.

This form of narrative grammar tries to grasp a single, but all-important, phenomenon: the action of plot-advance, "the simple and obvious fact that plots link together actions performed by the characters" (1985, 17). Concentrating on the step-by-step unfolding of the plot and focusing on the links between actions, the model succeeds in describing the phenomenon of plot-advance in an abstract, formal way, improving upon the earlier syntactic models of Propp and Bremond. In these earlier narrative grammars, events are more or less assembled like beads on a string without attending to the structural antecedents and consequences of events. In Pavel's model, events grow out of earlier problems and impose a vector, a direction, on later events: an incident is characterized as an event only if it affects the overall strategic situation. In this way the meaning of an event is emphasized: moreover, the model is elastic enough, in its basic three-part formula, to be applied to almost any narrative, unlike earlier grammars that consist of a multitude of very specific, concrete actions. On the other hand, in focusing on the syntax of plot events, the model is much more specific and concrete than the achronic, categorical taxonomies of Lévi-Strauss, Todorov, and Greimas.[7] In general, these theorists model events in a wholly abstract way, utterly dissolving the syntactic, step-by-step logic of plot in favor of a semantic emphasis that places plot events into categories defined by their oppositional or compatible features. The forward advance of plot syntax is ignored in these theories, as are the basic categories of actions and agency.

The potential problem of the Move structure departing radically from chronology and from presentational order is diminished in *1900*, for here most of the Moves are in fact "compact entities"; they not only follow a logical progression but also keep the chronology of the story and the order of presentation closely aligned. The film is characterized by a stable armature of strategic plot exchanges, probably because of its "referent," the historical order, which imposes a kind of generic system of regularities on the text. The logic of the Move structure follows the chronological order quite closely; as Barthes (1977) writes, consecutiveness could be passed off as causality here. In turn, the presentational order runs almost parallel to the chronological and the Move order. The presentational order, again owing to the generic requirement that the film model the historical order in a way that preserves a recognizable outline of events, cannot scramble the chronology overly much without sacrificing the regularity that gives the work its identity as a historical film.

Nevertheless, interesting deviations from straight chronological succession do occur in this film. The chief discrepancy in *1900* between the Move structure, the chronological order, and the order of presentation occurs in the *in medias res* opening of the film, and also in the case of the serial solutions to Move 7, solutions which, as I have indicated, are chronologically separated although they are logically condensed into one Move. Pavel addresses both types of discrepancy, adapting both to the Move model by way of what he calls, after Chomsky, "transformation rules."

He first addresses the problem of chronology, manifested in my treatment of the multiple Solutions to Move 7: "There are two ways of dealing with the non-coincidence between Move structure and chronology. One can postulate the necessity of chronological transformations . . . in which the order of events would be the chronologically correct one . . . (or) the moment when a given action takes place should be indicated by a time index" (1985, 35). The latter suggestion could be easily incorporated into our narrative tree for *1900*.

The *in medias res* transformation is of special interest for the modeling of *1900*, for it deals with the difference between presentational order and the Move structure:

> Among other things, transformations may account for the differences between the abstract order of events in the plot, which in my model is based on strategy, and the textual succession of represented events. Many narratives and dramas start *in medias res* . . . To open a poem or a play long after the beginning of the conflict means to present the reader or spectator with a strategic situation in which many, sometimes most of the Moves have already been performed, the load of the Problems unveiled, and the final race for a stable Solution set in motion. The transformation, *in medias res*, as it may be called, would thus search for the Move that takes place after a certain number of Problems have been presented, and a few provisional Solutions attempted. (Pavel 1985, 22–23).

Pavel's example is the story of Oedipus. The initial Move of the drama is the commission of parricide and incest by Oedipus. Yet this is not revealed until well after the second Move has been completed — the punishment of the gods seen in the plague on Thebes. Indeed, Move 1 is revealed to the reader in the middle of Move 3, which is Oedipus's attempt to deal with the Problem of the plague. Pavel's solution is to situate Move 1 under the Solution to Move 3, which respects the order of presentation. The ideal would then be to compare the purely logical structure of one tree with the adjusted structure of the other.

We can perform this *in medias res* transformation on the uppermost branches of the *1900* tree simply by moving the entire trunk over to the right, and placing it under the Solution to the Auxiliary line. As far as the order of presentation goes, this is where the flashback is introduced:

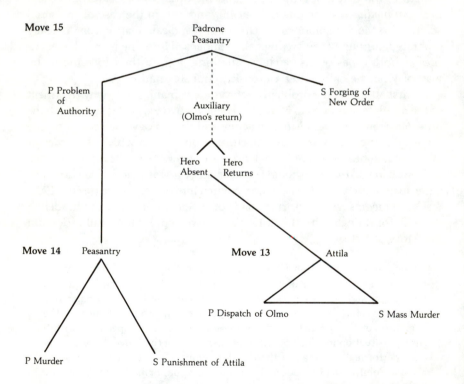

This arrangement would register the independence of the Moves of the Overture from the body of the work, and would show how the main narrative line rejoins the interrupted sequence at the point of the return of Olmo. It also reveals another important aspect of the narrative structure — the fact that the bulk of the narrative could be understood as unfolding under the Auxiliary line.

Although the Auxiliary line does not consititue the main line of development, we may nonetheless imagine a way in which the entire narrative tree could be rewritten with the emphasis on the Auxiliaries. We can quite easily project such a narrative line, with Olmo as Auxiliary indexing moves against Attila, the bad Auxiliary, which would effectively double the main plot line. In other words, the main line of the narrative could be rewritten as the story of Olmo, the Auxiliary, against Attila the Opponent. I have chosen to take my cue for the major polemical pair, however, from the Overture, with its clear-cut opposition between the peasantry and the bourgeoisie. Olmo and Attila thus serve mainly Auxiliary roles throughout the narrative, despite their textual prominence. Moreover, the Move structure without the *in medias res* transformation corresponds to our intuitive understanding of the plot, and to the way the protagonists would understand it.

Reflections on the Syntax of the Film

Thus we may say that the film proceeds in an "epic" fashion, with a nearly direct identity between the successive chronological order of the story, the order of presentation, and the progressive logic of the Move structure. As a modeling of history, the film could hardly be more straightforward. Apart from the interesting ramifications of the Overture, there is very little in the way of "creative deformation" of the fixed order of historical events. It is basically a linear history, which is explicitly evolutionist or developmental. In addition, it displays a strong repetitive pattern that links different sequences. Early plot sequences anticipate later ones, such as the repetition of the alliance between classes. The symmetrical arrangement of the Appeal for Help motif is also noteworthy. The two classes correspond to one another in their employment of this motif. The film as a whole fulfills the requirements of classical construction in its balanced, polemical arrangement of Moves and actants; its symmetry, which is displayed in the repetition of specific devices; and in its playing out of a kernel pattern in various narrative registers. It is teleological, in that the structure of the whole is immanent in all of its parts. The overall design that the historical assumes in the film is one of extreme regularity.

As one might expect in any history, death is one of its principal temporal markers, either initiating a new sequence or closing out a prior one. Each of the major transitions of the film is marked by death or the dispatch/ return of the Hero. What is camouflaged in the syntactic-logical level, however, is a certain symbolic imbalance in the quality of the Moves allotted to the cardinal characters. Using Bremond's distinction between the Agents and the Patients of the narrative, we can see that the Moves commanded by the peasantry are frequently of the Patient variety. Actions are imposed upon them, and they suffer the results of the tactics of others; nevertheless, they command the index because they are the group most affected by the Move. The Moves commanded by the bourgeoisie are active "violations of an accepted order" (with the exception of the Moves of the Overture), while those of the peasants are frequently types of "Lack." Also, the extended Tribulation of the peasantry is not matched by an extended Tribulation of the bourgeoisie, excepting the extended "trial" of Alfredo, who is held captive from the opening moments of the film. Additionally, the final Solution achieved by the peasantry is not definitive. It is the type of Solution that implies further Moves. The alliance with the Padrone, or with the new official "leader" of the liberation, does nothing to redress the imbalance throughout the film in the distribution of active roles. Furthermore, as demonstrated by the two previous alliances, this Solution seems remarkably weak and does not adequately function as a resolution for the film.

The syntactic analysis of the plot has proved useful for analyzing the regularities of its structure, its polemical patterns of opposition, and its method of articulating the historical event with the personal incident, employing the strongest possible narrative bond, the syntactic couplet of Problem and Solution. What it has made ambiguous, however, is precisely the density and variety of narrative worlds created by this coupling of the historical and the personal. The character who indexes such a Move becomes an exemplary composite, a kind of switching center for the two registers. The narrative worlds commanded by the different characters each convey a historical and psychological dimension. The broad semantic frame that was introduced to guide our reading at the syntactic level cannot register the diversity of narrative worlds produced by the text in linking private and public events through the device of the character-index. The co-presence of different narrative domains within the work can best be demonstrated through an analysis of the actantial level of the narrative, where it is evident that separate characters emerge from what amount to different genre systems. As we shift our attention to this level of the film, it will become clear that the strikingly orderly syntax of the plot provides a very stable armature for the projection of quite different narrative worlds, markedly unequal textual registers. The diversity of the text is possible only because of the gridwork of the plot design.

CHAPTER THREE

Analysis of the Character-System of *1900*

Despite the suggestion of boundless human depth and variety that is conveyed by the notion of the "character" in a narrative work, especially in the medium of the narrative film, the structural properties of the agents of narrative can be distilled into two complementary operations. Firstly, characters or actants work in tandem with the functional level of the plot to produce narrative events. Secondly, characters can be seen as "bundles of traits" that articulate the thematic and connotative material of the narrative. In Boris Tomashevsky's language, the character is seen as "a means of stringing the motifs together; and on the other [hand], he embodies the motivation which connects the motifs" (1965, 90). The first part of Tomashevsky's definition is structural and refers to the level of plot functions; the second is semantic, and refers to the general traits and beliefs of the character, Pavel's "set of maxims" governing character actions in relation to the fictional world. Formulated somewhat differently, we may say that the character ties the plot functions together and also anchors various semantic and symbolic fields of the text.[1]

The Theory of "Narrative Domains"

Extending Tomashevsky's definition a little, characters can be understood as commanding different "theaters of operation," different ideological and thematic zones of the narrative world. The premise for this view of character as a kind of delegate or emitting source for different messages about the narrative world can be found in Pavel, who writes that "plot based texts do not necessarily describe a homogeneous (imaginary) world. It rather appears that each narrative structure is divided into several *domains* centered around one or several main characters. These domains may display a great variety of properties. Notably, the domains of a single narrative work need not be governed by the same regularities" (1980, 105).

In *1900*, the characters are called upon to tie together, to constellate, a narrative universe of unusual variety and range. The separate zones or semantic domains associated with the various characters of *1900* are strikingly disparate, as if the text were partitioned into coterminous but contrary sectors: rather than a homogeneous imaginary world, the diegetic universe of *1900* consists of plural worlds, defined by very different systems of regularities. These different narrative domains center on the separate characters. Indeed, the textual partitioning of *1900* is so manifest that the characters of Attila and Olmo, for example, seem almost to belong to two different genres.

Originating from a very different perspective from Pavel's, the work of Frederic Jameson on actantial roles stresses the contradictory messages generated by the character-system of the text. Vastly simplifying his approach, we may say that the text dramatizes the deep social contradictions that animate it by setting up a closed system of thematic attributes, which the text "embodies" in various combinations. The text "rotates" these terms in an effort to find a resolution in a certain "ideal" type.[2] In these pages, I will unite Pavel's theory of distinct narrative domains, which emit contrary messages about the world of the text, with Jameson's notion of the character-system as the chief mechanism by which the text articulates and resolves its competing ideological messages. In both models for dealing with characters or actants, the narrative text is conceived as a divided, manifold, and heterogeneous structure, in which the lines of demarcation are most visible at the level of the characters. Likewise, both systems stress the semantic messages projected by the text, although Jameson will stress the contradictory nature of these messages.

A narrative domain, according to Pavel, is organized according to certain "propositions," or rules, governing the ontological, epistemological, axiological, and modal characteristics of the domain. He states that the concept of the narrative domain is founded on two narrative notions — the Move and the character. The notion of Move is a purely syntactic category; the notion of character, however, involves semantic consideration.

> [A] plot is split into more than one narrative domain, and is accordingly divided into several distinct sets of propositions. The nature of these propositions is heterogeneous. A domain contains ontological, epistemological, axiological and action propositions, summing, up, respectively, what is the case in that domain, what is known in it, what is good/better/bad/worse,

and what may/has to be done in that domain. Notice that I have omitted moral propositions, considering that some belong to the axiological set of propositions, while some others are included in the action-governing propositions . . . A work where all narrative domains contain identical sets of propositions is semantically homogeneous. Further classification yields works ontologically homogeneous, epistemologically homogeneous, etc. In contrast to these categories, one can talk of partitioned works, either globally or from a specific point of view. [Marlowe's] *Tamburlaine* for example, looks like an ontologically homogeneous and axiologically partitioned work: this means that the various domains (belonging to the main actors) function under the same ontological assumptions, but obey different axiological principles. (Pavel 1985, 45)

Narrative domains are related both to the syntax of plot — stressing the character or actant who indexes the Move — and to wider semantic considerations that are independent of the Move structure. Hence a character who anchors a domain need not be the same character who indexes the majority of Moves. This will have an important consequence in my analysis of the actantial level of *1900*, for we will find, at the outset, a rather striking disparity between the class protagonists of the Move structure — the peasantry versus the bourgeoisie — and the major actors controlling the narrative domains: the individual protagonists, Olmo, Alfredo, and Attila. At the characterological level, the focus of *1900* shifts to individuals, rather than classes. Pavel helpfully distinguishes between "plot-relevant semantic elements" and elements that constitute the "semantic focus" of the work: "It is unlikely, however, that all semantic elements . . . are plot-significant. A large category of semantic effects is based on the mere showing of things . . . Thus, even if it doesn't determine the shape of the plot, Tamburlaine's cruelty creates a semantic partition of the play into two "cells" . . . The cruelty of the hero towards his enemies belongs to the semantic focus of the play, without being plot-relevant" (Pavel 1985, 50–51).

Narrative Domains in *1900:* A Partitioned or Manifold Text

In *1900*, certain aspects of the narrative world are consistent throughout the range of characters and events. But other attributes of the narrative world are markedly inconsistent. For one, there seems to be something like an ontological division in the text. Temporal processes appear to differ, as if time imposed itself in a wildly variable manner. The Padrone Alfredo, for example, seems to be affected by time to a pronounced degree, while Olmo does not seem to age. In the peasant world, time is associated with the cycles of nature; the character Olmo, likewise, is really a kind of symbolic position or role in the text that is associated with the recurrent process of revolution. This is dramatized in the initial "arrest" of the Padrone by the adolescent revolutionary, who has adopted the name of Olmo as his "partisan name." We may now describe this curious feature of the narrative domain anchored by Olmo as a distinct ontological partition in the work, with separate ontological "rules" pertaining to the passage of time in Olmo's domain.

The temporal fluidity characteristic of the text attains a striking complexity when we compare its operation in the two domains anchored by Olmo and the Padrone. While the peasantry are in every way at a disadvantage in the narrative conflicts that structure the plot at the level of the Moves, there seems to be a compensatory and mitigating source of power in the ontological superiority evident in the peasants' relationship to time. This ontological superiority is expressed in a number of ways. It is most evident in the fact that the peasant characters no sooner die than they are replaced by physically identical types. This is the case with Olmo's wife, Anita, who is very quickly replaced by his daughter, Anita, who perpetuates the role of revolutionary firebrand. It is also seen in the reappearance of the Rigoletto character, bridging the gap between the pastoral scenes that open the film and the later period of persecution, as if the role and costume were continuous, preserved intact from generation to generation. The temporal uniqueness of the peasant world is also manifested by the fact that the forward progress of the narrative is countered by an insistent sense of repetition, especially in the daily rituals that organize this mode of existence. The film invokes the mood of repetition, rather than the actual display of it, by using the iterative narrative mode in conjunction with the peasant world. The reaping and the milking, the eating and the play, are presented as typical events, part of an ongoing series.

The iterative mood implies a temporality quite different from that of historical time. The iterative in fact contests with the historical order of one-time events that produce change. This conflict of narrative temporalities, in which an unchanging series of events suddenly encounters the historical, is most clearly expressed in the double-staging of the day of revolutionary triumph. Repetition is here associated with a new kind of history, as if history were not an incontrovertible order of events but an order that can be renewed and reformulated. The superior temporal reality of the peasantry is one of the key motifs of the film; symbolically, it can be extended to include the prophetic quality that Bertolucci associates with this way of life. Through this dilation of time, the peasant mode of

The world of the Padrones is one marked by ongoing decrepitude and loss. The bourgeois world seems to fade before our very eyes. Rather than being renewed through generational descent, the Berlinghieri family suffers a loss in vitality with each successive generation. (1990 Copyright © 1976 PEA Produzioni Europee Associate-Rome. All Rights Reserved. Courtesy of Paramount Pictures.)

production is rendered as both an ancient form of existence and as an anticipation of the future; it is seen as both a vestige of the agrarian past and as a desirable form for the ultimate, Communistic mode of production.

The world of the Padrones, on the other hand, is one marked by ongoing decrepitude and loss. The bourgeois world seems to fade before our very eyes, a decline most evident in the graduated weakness of the three characters who serially occupy the position of Padrone. Rather than being renewed through generational descent, the Berlinghieri family suffers a loss in vitality with each successive generation. The neurasthenic Padrone Alfredo is, at the end, hardly even a match for the young boy who calls himself Olmo. Time is clearly a corrosive force in the domain of the Padrone, with degeneracy and decline its inevitable consequences.

This difference in temporal processes is dramatized in a scene that is exceptionally lyrical in its rendering of the pastoral life. Early in the film, we witness a peasant celebration outdoors in a grove of trees. The peasants dance together in a somewhat ritualized country waltz to the music of ocarinas, clearly marking a kind of annual or seasonal rite. The camera tracks away from the collective celebration to focus on a little peasant girl in a boat on the river. She is being watched as well by the aged Padrone, who responds to her erotic appeal by making an open solicitation. The scene anticipates, in its sexual treatment of a child, the brutal sodomizing and murder of the young boy Patrizio by that perverse mirror of the bourgeois class, Attila. Here the eroticism is gentle, but the negative and despotic undercurrent of this type of exploitation, the *droit du seigner* held for generations by the Padrone, is clearly indicated. It is underlined by the motif of the little girl's shoes. Complaining about how hot her feet are, the little girl, Emma, mentions that her shoes originally belonged to Regina, who later becomes the monstrous wife of Attila, and who is an accomplice in the murder of Patrizio. Here, the little girl is hardly frightened or scandalized but rather seems to be amused. The old patriarch of the Berlinghieri clan cannot summon the requisite tumescence (the symbol of power), however, and regretfully dismisses the little girl. He then takes a length of chain and hangs himself.

The suicide of the Padrone clearly marks the passage from one historical period to another. Although the second Padrone will succeed the first, there is no sense of continuity or regeneration in this succession. It is rather a linear order that is here instantiated, in which death marks a radical shift to another dynastic period.

The peasant celebration, on the other hand, plainly represents a different relationship to time and history. Here the cyclical return of another season, the periodic repetition basic to the agrarian life, is seen as a continuous process of regeneration, symbolized by the turning patterns of the peasant waltz. The peasant world is associated with perpetual youth and growth, while the world of the bourgeoisie is associated with age, death, and the loss of vigor. The different temporalities operating in the two domains is emblematically rendered in this scene, as time operates within the two classes in a markedly contrary fashion.

This division of ontological rules regarding the action of time can also be extended to differences between the temporal organization of the domains of Attila and Olmo. Attila is full of malevolent plots and intentions; he lives only for the future. Olmo, on the other hand, lives fully in the present, oriented neither to the future nor to the past (although the peasant mode of production as a whole, as implied above, faces both directions). Olmo seems to exist in a state of pure potentiality. The difference between the domains of Attila and Olmo can be described in terms of the presence or absence of historical time in their separate domains. The character of the Fascist leader Attila is in a sense empowered by history, fueled by a vision of the malign future to which history appears to be leading. History is here seen, in Joyce's phrase, as "a long nightmare." Olmo, on the other hand, cannot command a plot oriented to the future;

Attila is full of malevolent plots and intentions: the character of the Fascist leader is fueled by a vision of the malign future to which history appears to be leading. History is here seen, in Joyce's phrase, as "a long nightmare." Bertolucci has called him "the summary concentrate of all the aggressive forces in the film." (1990 Copyright © 1976 PEA Produzioni Europee Associate-Rome. All Rights Reserved. Courtesy of Paramount Pictures.)

it is as if he pays for his agelessness with the absence of historical time in his domain. The prerevolutionary world of the peasantry may be invulnerable to the predations of time and age, but it is correspondingly limited to an existence founded on the present, devoid of a pragmatic vision of the future, and wholly lacking in a sense of the historical past. This makes the character of Olmo seem somewhat feeble in his encounters with Attila. His passivity and imperturbability are no match for Attila's ferocious pursuit of an imagined destiny.

These antagonistic structures of time and history comprise the principal ontological division of the work. The resolution of this division could be said to constitute the "project" of the film. The ahistorical temporality of the peasantry will be transformed, not into a linear historical effectivity, but into a quite different ontological mode in which the present will view the past as a prefiguration of a reality to be achieved in the future, a mode in which past, present, and future will be viewed neither in terms of linear history nor in terms of nature, but in terms of a unity that is social, a willing backward to empower the future.

I would like to stress the extreme novelty of this narrative division of the temporal register. Aside from supernatural tales or science fiction, I can think of no other plots that are characterized by time having heterogeneous features. Although the characters of 1900 inhabit the same spatial universe, the dimension of time operates upon the characters in a radically disparate fashion. Its coordinates are not uniform or constant, but protean. This is especially striking considering the topic of the film — the process of history. What might be called the "natural vector" of historical time becomes simply one more coordinate that the text can variously foreground, bracket, or completely countermand. In this textural rendering of history, the flow of historical time is no longer a determining force. The utopian transformation of the historical process may thus be said to involve the repudiation of the "inevitability" of linear historical time, subjecting time itself to a kind of plastic recomposition, a mode of historical consciousness that I described earlier as "genealogical."

In describing the properties of narrative domains, Pavel discusses, in addition to ontological characteristics, the epistemological features, governing what may be known about the domain; axiological features that indicate what is good, better, bad, or worse in a domain; and modal characteristics determining what may occur or will occur in a domain. A narrative may be consistent in some of its propositions and inconsistent in others. It may, for example, be consistent epistemologically, but inconsistent ontologically.

Such appears to be the case with *1900*. There are no major epistemological divisions, for example, as there might be in the case of a work such as *2001: A Space Odyssey*, with its very different epistemological worlds. In this work of science fiction, there is a radical epistemological disparity among the worlds commanded by HAL, the astronauts, and the extraterrestrials. In *2001*, HAL commands a good deal of knowledge that is inaccessible to the humans on board the spaceship "Discovery." In addition to his superior knowledge about the mission, HAL has access to the thoughts of the astronauts in a way that is not reciprocal. Conversely, the astronauts are completely baffled as to HAL's motivations. An even stronger division is apparent in the case of the extraterrestrials, signified by the sentient slab or obelisk. In the domain controlled by this superior intelligence, human actions, motivations, and the future of the human race itself seems absolutely transparent; known in advance, perfectly comprehended. The human characters, however, have only a glimmer of awareness of the existence of the other domain; it cannot be known or understood. In *1900*, however, the domains are equally accessible to one another epistemologically; they are uniform and consistent in their epistemic properties.

The axiological aspects of the text also appear to be consistent. *1900* does not describe a world of "topsy turvydom," in which what is good in one domain is bad in another and so on. Although actions vary in their valuation depending on the perspective from which they are seen, so that murder might be coded positively for the Villain and negatively for the Hero, this is merely a difference in perspective, rather than a fundamental reversal of the meaning of the event. An example of a true axiological partition can be found in a striking passage in Dante's *Inferno*. In the famous Ugolino episode, Dante has agreed to chip the frozen tears away from the eyes of Ugolino so that he may weep freely, if only Ugolino will recite his history. After hearing the ghastly tale, complete with Ugolino's description of his treason against his city and his cannibalizing of his children, Dante passes on without chipping the ice out of Ugolino's eyes, without keeping his part of the bargain. When Ugolino protests, Dante replies that it is a virtuous act to perpetrate a wrong, to defraud a soul so debased as Ugolino. This is a most dramatic reversal of axiological values, clearly showing a fundamental axiological partition between the domain of the Inferno and the familiar domain of the moral values that obtain in the earthly realm.

As stated before, no such axiological division exists in *1900*. It does not present a world in which values are inverted. But the force of evil is so profoundly exaggerated, unmatched by any corresponding scale of goodness or virtue in the film, that a certain axiological disparity or imbalance can be perceived. One world — Attila's — is entirely defined by evil, while Olmo's world seems curiously unmilitant in its goodness. As we shall see, this axiological disparity, where the range and intensity of values appear to be unequally apportioned, creates a very striking effect of imbalance that the text must work to "correct," much as the ontological antinomy described earlier must be rectified.

As for modal properties, which govern what may or can occur in a domain (formal logic defines the modal relations as possibility, probability, certainty, necessity, and obligation), we may say that they are consistent throughout the range of narrative domains in *1900*. An example of a divided modal universe can be found quite readily, however, in the world of silent, physical comedy. What may or can occur in the world of Buster Keaton will not hold for the other characters in the same film. For example, possibility, probability, and necessity are radically redefined by Keaton's unique repertory of billiard shots. Struck by Keaton's cuestick, billiard balls are induced to curve, weave, leap over obstacles, and suddenly brake to a stop. We can surmise that comedy regularly exploits modal concepts by emphasizing and subverting them in the same narrative structure, giving the comedian a different modal capacity. *1900*, however, places none of the modal relationships at issue and offers a consistent universe in terms of modal properties.

The chief divisions in the narrative world of *1900* can be found in the distinct ontological properties characteristic of the separate domains of the Padrone, Olmo, and Attila, and the vivid axiological imbalance between Olmo and Attila. It is obvious that the characters of *1900* operate in somewhat different worlds, an observation consistent with our intuitive sense that the film is composed of separate genre forms that seem to be highly incompatible but are nonetheless co-present in the artifact.

This sort of broad characterization of the spheres of action commanded by different characters establishes the principal features of the film as a partitioned world. Each character operates within quite different mediums, each of which possesses its own specific density and gravity. I will now chart the ways in which these characters interact, for the text does not preserve them as isolated entities, but interposes them in ways that affect the messages emanating from their domains.

Whereas Pavel's model is very useful for charting the differentiating features of particular narrative domains and for expanding the concept of the actant beyond its traditional definition — thus restoring the category of the character to a place of central importance in narratological analysis — it is essentially a static model in its present form of development. This is in marked contrast to the Move structure, which stresses the dynamic progression of plot advancement. One of the most deeply held laws of narrative form is surely the idea that a narrative process produces change or a modification in the fictional world. This change is not merely structural, as in a reconfiguration of the events, the characters, the setting, or the time period, but also semantic: narrative produces a change in the strategic significance of the events, in the status of the characters, in the qualities of the setting, and in the meaning of time in human affairs. The notion of semantic change or modification of the preexisting narrative world is poorly served by Pavel's model. What is needed is a way of linking the valuable insights provided by the theory of narrative domains with the process of dynamic modification of the fictional world. It can be shown that the partitioning of the text according to the properties associated with certain characters is merely the first step in this type of actantial analysis. The narrative text, in fact, seems to set up these individual domains only in order to exhange, cancel, or reorder their properties in the process of creatively reconstituting the narrative world.

The Semiotic Rectangle: Jameson's Adaptation of Greimas

Perhaps the best model for illustrating the semantic modification of the overall fictional universe through the interaction of different narrative domains is Jameson's adaptation of Greimas's semiotic rectangle. As we shall see, this model can be productively articulated with the theory of narrative domains. In Greimas's system, the four-part mapping of the symbolic universe of the text into opposed and allied terms comprises the entire range of semantic possibilities within the work. In Jameson's hands, it is used to register the ideological contradictions of the text and the process of exchange by which they are resolved. Jameson writes that the rectangle "is designed to diagram the way in which, from any given starting point . . . , a whole complex of meaning possibilities, indeed, a complete meaning system, may be devised . . . Greimas' rectangle is thus essentially an articulation of the traditional logical concept of the contradictory and the contrary" (1972, 164).

The semiotic rectangle consists of a major opposition, or set of contraries, and a minor opposition, deriving from the contradictories of the two major terms. The standard example is between good and evil. The single term good implies its opposite, or contrary, evil. The negations or contradictions of these two cardinal terms are also logically implied and form the minor opposition, non-good and non-evil.

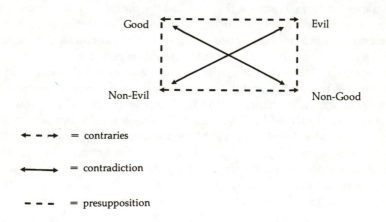

Good and evil are contraries, while good and non-good are contradictories, actual negations of each other. Additionally, the relation between good and non-evil is one of presupposition. From a single term, a whole range of possibilities is thus generated. For Jameson, this range comprises the terms of the ideological closure of the text, the limits beyond which the text cannot go.

The various characters of *1900* project combinations of semantic attributes that can be usefully mapped according to this model. We have already seen how the text presents its characters as overt representatives of larger dominions, such as the association of the peasantry with nature and the bourgeoisie with history. But these large themes or messages are intersected by "personalized," psychological characteristics of the actors. The result is a kind of composite: the character becomes not a psychological facsimile but rather a kind of switching center of public and private themes and messages, all of which revolve around the central contradiction perceived in the divided semantic fields associated with the two classes in opposition. The antinomic pair, peasantry and bourgeoisie, communicate a host of attributes, a "collection of traits," that are embodied in the various characters in different combinations. Moreover, this central oppositional pair can be conceived as surface-structure labels for the deeper opposition of nature and history. The semantic closure of the text consists in the rotation of these traits so that an "ideal synthesis," or resolution, of the central oppositional terms results. The semantic and ideological closure of the work can be initially sketched as a four-part system, represented in the model below:

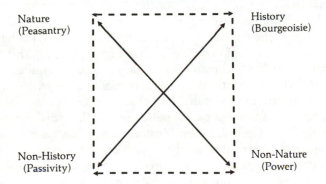

Here the minor opposition comprised of the negative terms has been filled in with a positive content and given a concrete meaning, passivity versus power, providing the system with a greater quality of significance. The premise of the model is that the entire semantic field of the text can be generated from a single term, nature, which gives birth to a set of allied and opposing terms. I will describe the contradictory of nature, the domain of the peasantry, as power, a quality specifically lacking in the peasant world. On the other hand, the contradictory of history, the domain of the bourgeoisie, will be designated as passivity, a quality antithetical to the bourgeois Agents of history. The minor opposition formed by the terms passivity versus power constitutes a clear-cut set of contraries. The relation between passivity and the peasantry is one of presupposition, as is the relation between power and the bourgeoisie.

These terms and groupings are useful in describing the character-system of the text in terms of its underlying symbolic logic. The different characters can be mapped according to this system in a straightforward and illuminating way. Olmo, representing the peasant class, quite clearly embodies the world of nature: he is associated with the earth in a most picturesque fashion. He wears a crown of writhing frogs throughout the opening scenes. Later, he is shown skillfully slaughtering hogs and bestowing the gift of a warm liver upon a friend. Toward the end of the film, he is portrayed working the anus of his horse in order to stimulate the production of feces, which he then plasters onto the face of the Fascist leader Attila. Moreover, he is sexually robust and is associated with procreation and potency.

But Olmo also embodies the negative term of passivity. Many times he acquiesces in his lifelong struggle with the bourgeoisie and with Attila. His brutal treatment at the hands of the Fascists is never repaid in kind, never avenged. Although the semes or messages of nature and passivity that circulate in the text are projected in the form of a character, an "anthropomorphic nucleus," to borrow a phrase from Jameson, this character is in many ways less a human subject than a kind of symbolic position in the text. What is sacrificed is a certain quality of psychological credibility in the portrait of the individual character. Olmo's lack of response to provocation is simply not quite believable on the individual level. But in his embodiment of a class and historical position he expressly illustrates the larger historical issue: the separation of the peasantry from the axis of history and power. This is precisely the issue or problem posed by the text. The resolution of the narrative will consist in the rotation of the terms so that the peasantry is no longer associated with passivity; another character or group of characters will be found to occupy this position. The text will generate various combinations in the form of characters in an effort to find an ideal synthesis, a resolution of the central opposition of nature and history.

The character of Attila is associated throughout the film with the malign forces of history and power. He is first introduced as the foreman presiding over the industrialization of the farm; later, he becomes a leader of the Blackshirts. Identified with a kind of negative historical process, Attila is quite clearly a species of "antinature"; moreover, he is portrayed as sexually perverse, in contrast to Olmo's "natural" sexuality. Attila, however, does not occupy the axis of history and power throughout the film; he attains increasing stature as the story unfolds, but he commands this cardinal position only after this axis has been vacated by the traditional authority figure of the bourgeois class, the Padrone.

In effect, Attila gradually takes over the role the Berlinghieris had commanded for generations. The eclipse of Alfredo, the third Padrone, reveals the progressive logic, the generative properties of the film. We can plainly see how the film registers historical change in terms of a closed, dynamic system. The earlier Padrones, in contrast to Alfredo, quite clearly occupied the axis of history and power. Alfredo, however, is the weakest of the three successive Berlinghieris. Although he is associated with progress and with the modern world in general, he is himself incapable of producing positive change. Although he subscribes to a version of the "master narrative" of bourgeois progressivism, he nevertheless presides over the loss of the world he has inherited. And although he maintains his economic status, he cedes influence and authority to Attila. Moreover, he fails to produce an heir and thus fails to project the Berlinghieri line into the latter half of the twentieth century.

In short, Alfredo is displaced from his familial and class position as the embodiment of history and power. He is eclipsed by Attila, who supplants him on the stage of history. This Fascist terrorist, as he acquires status and wealth, passes himself off as a member of the bourgeoisie — the new embodiment of a historical order based on force. Alfredo's position in the text thus changes dramatically. He comes to occupy the register of the "neutral term," embodying the minor opposition, power and passivity. Detached from the new historical order of the Fascists and the peasantry alike — separated from both the malignant and the visionary history represented in the text — the Padrone retains a symbolic position in the film as a kind of residual power figure, but one that is effectively neutralized, passive. We might say that the "character," the "anthropomorphic nucleus," the "person" of Alfredo can be disjoined from the class and historical position of the Padrone. What we discerned "intuitively" in the case of Olmo — that he is less a human subject than a vessel for class and historical messages — we can articulate precisely in the case of Alfredo. His class, his historical role can be divided from his private, psychological dimension: together, they cancel one another out, forming the "neutral term" of the rectangle. The rotation of terms disclosed by the use of the semiotic rectangle reveals the way the text has transformed the narrative domain of the character Alfredo, in effect producing a "split subject" that could not exist before a set of semantic exchanges had been completed. Following these exchanges, the character-system can be represented in the fashion below:

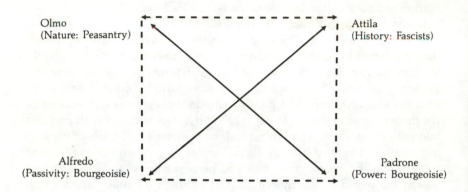

The "complex term" or ideal synthesis of the two major terms of the opposition remains, however, the most daunting challenge of the narrative system I have devised. The combination of history and nature seems unable to be embodied in any one character. It might be said to be anticipated in the figures of the two ancient patriarchs who preside over the opening scenes of the film. Viewing these two characters as essentially one, we find that they do combine the semes of history and nature. Both men are portrayed as robust, partaking of a "natural" sexuality. Each is closely tied to the land and has a sense of posterity and the passing of a historical era. In the text, however, each patriarch exists only as a kind of mirage or phantasm of some Edenic period "before the revolution." The ideal synthesis that together they represent must be seen not as a realized, prior historical state, but rather as an anticipation of the utopian culmination to which the film continually points. This doubling of characters is reproduced at the end of the film as well. Olmo and Alfredo are paired in the final coda in an overtly allegorical tableau representing the fractious union of the two classes, peasantry and bourgeoisie. Bertolucci has said that these two figures represent "two sides of the same personality," and that together they can help us "peep into the inner structures of the century" (1975, 15). But it seems to me that the complex synthesis that the text demands can only be attained through the intervention of some properly utopian transformation that will be associated most profoundly with the narrative domain of the character Olmo. In order to render this transformation, we must attempt a more complete synthesis of the two models than we have done so far.

The Synthesis of the Two Models:
Narrative Domains and the Semiotic Rectangle

The transformation of the domain of Olmo's character from nature to that ideal combination of nature and history designated as the utopian marks the profound wish-fulfilling or revolutionary projection of the text. This position represents a kind of horizon figure, beyond which the text cannot go. As Jameson writes in another context: "he blocks out a place which is not that of empirical history, but of a possible alternate one . . . [History] is thus emptied of its finality, its irreversibility, its historical inevitability, by a narrative register which offers it to us as a mere conditional history" 1981, 168–69). This transformation involves a sweeping shift in narrative registers, one in which empirical history and the notion of phenomenal nature are decisively recoded as utopian.

The return of Olmo at the moment of revolutionary triumph will mark the transition to the utopian resolution of the film. The properties of the domain associated with Olmo — the absence of temporal decay, the sense of a perpetual present time, striking passivity in the face of manifest provocation (all of which correspond to the domain of nature) — are here consummated in the transition to the utopian. Olmo's immunity to the negative effect of temporal processes can be read as the translation of historical time into the perpetual regenerative time of an exalted nature.

Without descending into impressionism, we can describe this semantic transformation of the domain anchored by Olmo as precisely the merging of the two antinomic terms, nature and history, which the text has associated with different "cells" of the narrative universe. These two cells are endowed with different ontological configurations and with different axiological scales of value. The ontological partitioning of the text, for example, results in a narrative world in which time operates differently, and in which death receives a different encoding in each of the two domains. The axiological partition results in a disparity of scale in which evil is associated with power while good is associated with passivity, thus letting evil and power go unchecked. The semantic transformation of the text will involve the crossing-over of these terms — the perpetual temporality of Olmo's domain will suddenly be shown to control and encapsulate historical time, rather than being divided from historical time, and the axiological imbalance will be rectified by the empowering of passivity, the translation of passivity into power.

But this transformation involves the projection of another textual register, for at the level of the manifest text, the Villainy role is aggrandized in the film, made exorbitant, while the Hero role is progressively diminished. The order of history, correspondingly, seems to belong solely to the repertory of the villainous Attila. Above all, the transformation of Olmo's domain must restore the Hero to prominence, for it appears as if the Villain, rather than the Hero, is installed at the center of the film.

The Villainy function, aligned with history, maintains a commanding place throughout the text. The various heinous acts of Attila serve as temporal markers for the Fascists' rise to power. Without a redemptive Hero, history is painted as a sadomasochistic spectacle. The text's concentration on the demonic violence of Attila, who commits his worst crimes on the occasions of civic and religious celebrations—the wedding of the Padrone, Christmas Eve, etc.—calls for a stronger response than that supplied by Olmo. Indeed, the decisive moment of partisan triumph and revolutionary breakthrough is marked, in its first enactment, by the absence of the Hero. In its second enactment, there is a corresponding absence of the Villain, Attila, who is executed before Olmo returns from exile. The partitioning of these two domains is so rigorously maintained that the two characters belong to two distinct theaters of operation. The actantial roles of Opponent and Hero are conspicuously separated throughout the film and absolutely segregated in the two versions of the revolutionary moment represented at the beginning and the ending of the film.

Seen in this light, the actantial and axiological disequilibrium between Villain and Hero might stem from the ideological necessity to bracket the Hero's role in the Marxian epic, symbolic requirements altering the deep-structural relations. The Hero function, accordingly, is to be translated into the Auxiliary function, as Olmo becomes, not the avenger of Attila's crimes, but the bookish bearer of the revolution.

In order to arrive at the "complex term"—the synthesis of nature and history—the text must summon another semantic frame, which is absent from the manifest structures of the text but present by logical implication. The hyperbolization of the Villainy function, which creates an axiological imbalance, provides the key to this latent dimension. In Georges Bataille's reading of Sade, it is precisely a similar emphasis on villainy and transgression that points to an antithetical structure by insistently calling forth the absent domain of the Sacred. Bataille finds that the scenes of ritual deviancy that structure the Sadeian text highlight this absent dimension, which assumes the status of the nonrepresentable figured only by its opposite, by the invocation of the diabolical and perverse. In *1900*, the predominance of the motifs of Villainy and transgression and the complete partition of the two narrative domains suggests a similar structuring absence, a similar coded appeal to another order of discourse, a similar kind of theological inversion.

Lest this formulation appear too mystical, it is important to ground our reading securely in the theories of the text. In a study closely related to Pavel's, Lubomir Dolezel posits the concept of an invisible narrative domain as a structuring device in the novels of Kafka. The world described in *The Trial*, for example, is dominated by the invisible, omnipotent domain of the Courts. Characters from the visible, ordinary world cannot enter into the Courts and can obtain no real knowledge of their workings; yet the Courts maintain an absolute hegemony over life in the phenomenal, daily world of Josef K. A similar structure can be found in *The Castle*, where the domain of Count Westwest exerts a powerful and unidirectional influence on the events occurring in the everyday world of the Village.

This concept can be usefully applied to the problem of the transformation of Olmo's domain. It provides a perspective that allows us to rewrite or recode the curious temporality of this domain, and its valuation of passivity, under the rubric of the utopian. For the negative invisible world of Kafka's fiction, we will substitute the positive invisible world of the utopian. It is a powerful semantic current of the work that can be shown to have a determining effect on the meaning of the text. The invisible narrative domain of the utopian gives to Olmo's return the quality of a salvific intervention, producing an almost Christological association that had earlier been invoked only negatively through Attila. More importantly, this invisible narrative domain changes the meaning of the term "history" in the text.

With history seen in the light of the utopian, in the light of an all-embracing unity that substantially recodes the events of linear, historical time, the destiny of the characters comes to be read as the destiny of the entire human race. This is not an unfamiliar perspective for historical fiction to assume. As Jameson has written in another context, it is similar to the anagogical level of medieval interpretation, which he finds subtends many works of an ostensibly historical nature. The anagogical can be understood as "the collective meaning of history; from the story of a particular earthly people the anagogical narrative is transformed into universal history, the destiny of human kind as a whole" (Jameson 1981, 30–31).

The anagogical or utopian level, which can only emerge in *1900* through a combination of the terms history and nature, is brought into relief in the final scenes. It is first signified overtly in the shot that initiates the second rendering of the Day of Liberation. As the sound of peasant singing is heard on the soundtrack, the camera tracks around a big elm tree (iconically invoking the character Olmo, whose name means elm tree) to reveal an elderly man exercising his voice amid the thunder of artillery and the smoke of bursting shells. This shot can be taken as a kind of signal for the transformation of Olmo's domain into the synthesis of nature and history that constitutes the utopian resolution of the text. The "singing elm tree" also seems to echo the boyhood incident when Olmo "listened for his father's voice" by putting his ear against the pole of a telegraph line.

The final scenes center on the return of Olmo after an absence of several years and on the celebration that follows the partisan victory, which Bertolucci describes as the flowering of a peasants' utopia. Here, the text unveils a striking symbol of the fusion of history and nature to which the text has been leading. In a kind of Chinese Red Ballet celebration, the peasant women unearth a huge red banner they had buried and parade it around the square, commenting that "It just got bigger every year." The banner explicitly mingles the natural and historical orders—the periodic cycle of growth and renewal and the birth of revolutionary consciousness. Furthermore, this symbol can be linked to Olmo, and to his domain, for in an earlier passage in the film detailing his childhood, he is shown "screwing the earth"; this gesture, in conjunction with the red banner brought out from underground, can be read, in the associative logic of the film, as the insemination of the earth with revolutionary purpose, bringing together the symbology of the natural and the historical orders.

But it is in the closing moments of the film, in a scene that functions as a coda, that the domain of the utopian comes most fully into view. Olmo and Alfredo here seem to occupy a universe in which past, present, and future are simultaneous. The ontological features we noticed earlier regarding the operation of time in Olmo's domain are fully realized as the film uses rapid flashbacks, intercutting past and present fluidly, to convey a sense of simultaneity. Images of the characters as old men are connected to images of their youthful selves. As the moment of the deaths of the two characters is staged, the film dwells on the images of childhood. The coda links the death of the characters to the history of the century in such a way that history is seen, finally, as a regenerative force, leading to renewal and rebirth.

Reflections on the Model

The actantial analysis confirms a pattern already visible in the Move structure—the fact that the individual antagonists, Olmo and Attila, do not compete directly, but instead occupy separate narrative worlds. This is seen in the Move structure insofar as they function simply as Auxiliaries for the separate "camps" and do not index Moves in a polemical arrangement against each other: they compete only through their clients, the peasantry and the bourgeoisie, and thus are never brought into direct contact at either level of the text.

The most significant advantage of the synthesis I have undertaken is that the model of narrative domains can now be dynamized through use of the semiotic rectangle and, conversely, the terms of the semiotic rectangle can be defined more concretely by using the ontological, epistemological, axiological, and modal values that make up and distinguish the separate narrative domains. The combined model has illuminated the global oppositions structuring the work and has revealed the way the central conceptual antinomy of nature versus history is refigured in the exchange of positions, attributes, and values associated with the characters. Moreover, the association of the utopian with an invisible narrative domain seems to me to be an effective way of approaching this level of the text, which would seem on its surface to be inaccessible to narrative analysis. Above all, what the model demonstrates is that the characters, far from being subordinate to plot actions as has been argued in narrative theory, are in fact composites of all the thematic and symbolic systems in the text. Without descending to the naive humanism that would regard the characters as human facsimiles, we may say that the character-system constitutes the nodal center of the semantic universe projected by the text. Thus, the character-system can be reintroduced into narrative analysis as one of the most complex elements of the text. In the case of *1900*, the analysis reveals the transformation of the narrative domains associated with Olmo and Alfredo to be an essential feature of the film's historical project and discloses the density and multiplicity of narrative worlds created by the coupling of fictional characters and historical events.

INTRODUCTION TO CHAPTERS FOUR, FIVE, AND SIX

Tense, Mood, and Voice

In the following three chapters, I will explore the three registers of narrative structure treated by Genette in *Narrative Discourse*. These consist of the categories of tense, mood, and voice, which Genette draws from verb grammar. Tense, in narratology, refers to the temporal relations between the abstract level of the story and the concrete, artistically ordered level of the narrative. Mood refers to the modalities of distance and perspective: how much or how little information is given, and from what perspective. In contemporary usage, the category of mood has been largely replaced by the category of focalization: the study of the degree and manner in which an event is filtered through a specific character's perception; the question of distance and perspective here becomes a question of how specific characters function as reflectors — screens or filters of the narrative events. The category of voice, on the other hand, refers to the narrator's own commentary, judgment, or overt interpolations in the relating of the fiction. The distinction between mood and voice — which is frequently blurred in older uses of the term "point of view" to describe both functions — can be understood as a distinction between "Who sees?" and "Who speaks?" or between the narrative perspective that provides an "angle of vision" on the events and the narrative "voice" that tells the story. In my treatment of the category of voice, the textual figures of moving camera and parallel editing will be taken as instances in film of narrative voice, instances of expressive interpolation on the part of the narrator.

Chapters four, five, and six can thus be seen as a kind of conceptual group. Following Genette, most treatments of narrative form, such as those by Mieke Bal and Shlomith Rimmon-Kenan, emphasize the interdependence of these three categories. While the three categories are distinct and in fact belong to different "levels" of narrative structure, they reinforce one another in a different way from the more autonomous functioning of the syntax of plot and the semantic generation of characters. Perhaps most importantly, the three registers have in common their dependence on textual properties: where the analysis of the syntax of plot and the character-system sought a more abstract, or deep-logical, system of articulation, tense, voice, and mood are wholly expressed through the details of textual design. We will thus shift our attention away from the abstract modeling of deep-structural relations to the phenomenal surface of the text, not to disclose its formal design as an object of study in its own right, but to analyze the narrative hierarchies and voices, the narrative messages harbored within the architecture of narrative form.

CHAPTER FOUR

Temporality as
Historical Argument in *1900*

Every great historical narrative is an allegory of temporality.
— Hayden White (1985, 181)

In *1900* the relations of tense — defined by Genette as order, duration and frequency — convey a complex historical argument, serving as analogues to such traditional historiographic techniques as cause and effect analysis and linking of the particular and the general. Moreover, the film essays a mode of historical causation through its codes of temporality that may be called genealogical or archaeological. Historical occurrences are ordered and analyzed in the narrative not as elements in an immutable sequence of events but rather as if they were episodes in an "unfinished plot" whose meaning is not fixed; the past is apprehended as open and responsive to the present and the future, conceived as containing the "conditions of possibility" leading to the film's utopian resolution. It is in its temporal features that the film manifests its alternative approach to historical cause and the historical order most directly.

In employing the concept of genealogy to describe the film's historical method, I am adopting the modified account of Michel Foucault's model set forth by Jameson and White. While differing from Foucault in its emphasis on the narrative trajectory of the historical process, this modified genealogical approach retains Foucault's rejection of the idea of the past having imposed a predetermined form on the present. The model thus opposes the finality, the suprahistorical perspective of a traditional historiography that "assumes the existence of immobile forms" and reduces the "diversity of time into a totality" (Foucault 1977, 146).

Rather than viewing the past as a fixed and determined order that has developed in a linear and inevitable way into the present — a genetic approach characteristic of many historical films — *1900*, consistent with its

Marxian orientation, comprehends the historical past as a potential re-
source for the present, and as a set of possibilities that can be fulfilled
in the future. As White explains: "human beings can will backward as well
as forward in time; willing backward ocurs when we rearrange accounts
of events in the past that have been emplotted in a given way, in order
to endow them with a different meaning or to draw from the new emplotment reasons for acting differently in the future . . . we can regard this
change in perspective as a causal force in history, effecting changes in past
ages' conception of their natures" (1987, 150). White points out that the
past is affected most manifestly in the case of revolutionary societies,
which may undertake to rewrite their histories from a new political perspective, emphasizing events that had previously appeared unimportant,
grasping them now as prefigurations of the new social order providing the
ground and the possibility of a "new kind of action" in the future.

In reading *1900* in this fashion, I am directly opposing the view of Robert Kolker concerning the film's historical orientation: "within the context
of the fiction, the revolution cannot be permitted to endure. By the end
of *1900* Bertolucci seems to become weighted down by historical reality . . . There was no communist revolution [in Italy after the war] . . .
By choosing a realist form with which to present this history, Bertolucci
is forced to end his film in an impasse" (1985, 201). But Kolker here ignores the film's political call to keep the story open and alive, its express
foregrounding of a perspective on the past that, while remaining within
the conventions of realism, resists the kind of closure he describes. Far
from ending in an impasse, the film asserts that the moment of struggle
is not set firmly in the past—the point of the ending is precisely to reorient
the perspective that views the moment for effecting change to be over. It
is not, as Kolker has it, that "Since history—up to the point of the film's
making—can resolve nothing, Bertolucci chooses to close his film with
nothing resolved; or worse" (1985, 201), but rather that closure and resolution belong only to a story than can be told retrospectively. *1900* instead
views the past as a story yet to be completed.

Bertolucci has stressed that the film concerns the birth of historical consciousness in the peasantry and that the climactic event of the film, the
Italian Day of Liberation, provides the perspective for the film's overall
treatment of history, a history that includes an anticipatory expression of
the future: "It's a day, the 25th of April, 1945 . . . and it includes the
whole century. We took it as a sort of symbolic day on which is unleashed, on which flowers this peasants' utopia . . . this day of utopia
contains the century . . . the premise of this day lies in the past, but the
day also contains the future" (Bertolucci 1975, 12). Although this descrip-

tion might appear to deviate from any realistic or historical interpretation of the past, situating the film firmly in the sphere of allegory rather than that of historiography, it is grounded in the historical approach of Antonio Gramsci—originally cited as a model for the film by Bertolucci—who stresses the concrete effectivity of such an orientation: "If one applies one's will to the creation of a new equilibrium among the forces which really exist . . . one still moves on the plane of effective reality . . . What 'ought to be' is therefore concrete; indeed, it is the only realistic and historicist interpretation of reality, it alone is history in the making and philosophy in the making, it alone is politics" (1971, 172).

The theoretical and historical argument of the film can be grasped most readily in its temporal figures. Employing the major subcategories of tense, i.e., order, duration, and frequency, in a highly symbolic fashion, the film uses the structures of temporality as analogues to historical argument. The actual historical events the film treats are in a sense examined and interpreted through a symbolic repatterning of the chronological continuum.

While temporal complexity is characteristic of Bertolucci's work, establishing the symbolic matrix of such films as *The Conformist, The Spider's Stratagem*, and *The Last Emperor*, the relations of tense are placed in bold relief in *1900*. The political message of the film ultimately emerges in this figurative or poetic form, as the meaning of historical events and of temporal experience is discovered not in concrete occurrences but in a kind of historical consciousness, evoked by creating a multidimensional picture of time, that sees the past as subject to a change in perspective, open to a reordering, a "willing backward" as well as forward.

Order

It has been frequently observed that deviations of order are quite rare in the cinema. As Brian Henderson writes: "It seems that the majority of films of every era have been told in straight chronological order whereas, according to Genette, such order is the exception among novels" (1983, 5). With no built-in tense system to indicate the transition to the past or to express the shift from present to future, cinema must rely on a battery of cues involving many different "channels of signification"—including voice-over, graphic titles, optical and acoustic effects, a change in costume and locale—in order to signify a change to another temporal frame. When an anachrony is employed in film, it is generally a flashback, or analepsis, rather than the very unusual flashforward, or prolepsis.

Direct, linear chronology is usually employed in the historical film, presumably to reinforce the link between consecutiveness and causality, which, as Barthes reminds us, is the "mainspring" of narrative activity: "that very confusion between consecution and consequence, what comes after being read in a narrative as what is caused by" (1977, 94). As Sorlin writes concerning patterns of explanation in historical films: "A caused B which caused C . . . We are so familiar with this type of direct, linear causality that we might think it is a characteristic of all films" (1980, 210).

Historical films that do deviate from linear chronology tend to introduce a more complex model of causality. A case in point is Bertolucci's recent *The Last Emperor*, which utilizes numerous analepses to link the framing story of Pu Yi's reeducation under the Communist party to the earlier events of his life. Here, historical causation seems to operate on a parallel track to the events of the plot; Pu Yi is insistently portrayed not as the Agent but as the Patient of historical processes: the film stresses his hermetic removal from history, in the conventional sense. But at the climax of his reeducation, a dramatic shift in perspective occurs: he is shown to be the very exemplar of the changed historical order, the embodiment of "history in the making."

Whereas the conjunctural logic characteristic of historical films emphasizes the immediate cause, or else renders indirect cause as if it were immediately operative, the shuttling back and forth in time in *The Last Emperor* serves explicitly to insert the past into the cultural revolution of the present. Historical causation is here seen as the product of the will to create Gramsci's "new equilibrium among the forces which really exist" (1971, 172). The deviations in order mark the construction of a history that has ceased to be a history of events. Instead, it concentrates on the confrontation between past and present; in the person of Pu Yi, the past will be brought to the present and changed. The goal of this confrontation is precisely to make Pu Yi the historical figure he never was in life. In becoming a "model citizen," the character brings into view and fulfills an entire historical process. From this perspective, he encapsulates most of the stages of Chinese history, from monarchy to republicanism to Fascism to Communism. It is a narrative of emergence built on a polemical exchange.

What is most unusual in this modeling of history is that the past acquires significance only as part of a theoretical practice in the present, as part of an ongoing polemic between past and present. Rather than attempting to fashion a new, more adequate representation of the past, the film asserts that the practice of historiography is one of criticism and confrontation — of the present with the past, of one social form or mode of production with another.

109

Bertolucci fashions this critique largely through the narrative device of anachrony, interrupting the story of the past at strategic points for clarification and criticism, refusing to allow the notion of historical cause to appear to emerge organically from the "logic of events," insisting that the attribution of causal elements be suspended, interrogated, made one with a concept of "history in the making"—in other words, made one with the practice of politics.

1900, on the other hand, appears to emphasize the conjunction of events in its analysis of historical cause. It follows a more or less straightforward order, with only two deviations—both flashbacks—occurring at the beginning and at the end. This generally straightforward sequencing of events, in the words of Kolker, creates "the illusion of being historically determined" (1985, 77). But the two deviations in order that do occur, and the emphasis they receive in the text, are highly significant to the film's complex modeling of the historical process.

This is especially visible in the relationship between the Overture of the film and the first scene of its main story. The historical significance of the Overture is underlined by a title card, which reads simply, "Northern Italy; April 25, 1945. The Day of Liberation." The title card indicates that this date will exert a telling pressure on the rest of the film: but whether this date should be taken as initiatory or conclusive concerning the historical events the film will treat is left ambiguous. The frame of importance provided by the title card communicates a double message: the scene functions both as the crystallized expression of historical conflicts that have been building for decades and as the heralding of a new order, one that contains the future in an embryonic form.

The special kind of causality at work in *1900* is exemplified in this opening sequence. The film begins not with the birth of the two main characters, but with the culminating event of its historical chronicle, the "Day of Liberation." This scene details the last violent moments of struggle against the Fascists and the Padrone who has supported the cruel regime. The message of the Overture emerges clearly in the confrontation between the boy partisan, one of the peasants oppressed for generations by the landowning Berlinghieri family, and the aging Padrone. The Padrone has been "captured" by the peasant boy and is being held at gunpoint. He attempts to bribe the boy, asking him if he would like to visit America "with his master." The boy responds: "There are no more masters!" With this declaration the Overture is concluded. Following this, the long flashback that comprises the body of the film begins. The boy's statement thus serves as a kind of epigraph or motto announcing the film's principal historiographic theme, setting forth the orientation that will de-

The Padrone has been "captured" by the peasant boy and is being held at gunpoint. He attempts to bribe the boy, asking him if he would like to visit America "with his master." The boy responds: "There are no more masters!" The boy's statement serves as a kind of epigraph or motto announcing the film's orientation. (1990 Copyright © 1976 PEA Produzioni Europee Associate-Rome. All Rights Reserved. Courtesy of Paramount Pictures.)

termine its approach to the past, guiding our reading of the flashback that follows.

Like the vanishing point of a perspective drawing, the historical process will lead, the film argues, to the decisive moment when such a statement embodies the historical reality. The film here asserts the governing principle informing its treatment of history: from this cardinal point, the past will be viewed as a set of possibilities enabling this moment of fulfillment. The opening scene thus invites us to view the signs of the historical from two perspectives: from the specific moment in Italian history when this condition was briefly realized, and from the perspective of the future when these events may appear as precursors to an achieved historical end.

Directly after the phrase "There are no more masters!" which concludes the Overture, a second graphic insert bridges the transition between the events of 1945 and the long analepsis that comprises the body of the film. The title card reads simply, "Many years before . . .". This nebulous title presents a strong contrast to the specificity of the first title, in a sense softening the historical designation in favor of a fairy-tale positioning of time, preparing the viewer for the mixture of historical and fictional in

111

the film. The personal stories of Alfredo, the future Padrone, and Olmo, the future peasant leader, will be developed in a past that is nostalgic rather than historical; but this past is nevertheless surrounded, hedged in, and indeed openly invaded by the history rattling outside.

The two title cards alert us to the fact that the embedded pastoral sequence comprising the childhood of the two characters will eventuate in the historical events of 1945. The historical thus provides the frame for the narrative. But the earlier, fairy-tale past provides the explanation. The title "Many years before . . . " signifies not only a transition, but the promise of a causal explanation, as if this idyllic past could reveal the root causes for the revolutionary events depicted in the prologue.

This shift in order is significant not only because it highlights the thread of a guiding historical argument but, more importantly, because is justifies and motivates the events we have just witnessed. The repatterning of chronology, coupled with the use of two title cards that invoke very different codes of explanation, can be interpreted as a kind of commentary. The promise of an explanation signified by the restructuring of the chronological continuum goes well beyond the requirement of making the events intelligible: it endows the events with an ethical dimension. This is reinforced by the appeal to a past that is universal rather than specific, typical rather than unique—a message communicated by the phrasing of the second title card. It marks the intersection of an overall theory of history with the notion of individual and class action.

The juxtaposition of different temporal moments, taken out of sequence and reordered according to a discursive narrative logic, serves to legitimize the peasants' actions. As White comments: "If every fully realized story . . . is a kind of allegory, points to a moral, or endows events, either real or imaginary, with a significance that they do not possess as a mere sequence, then it seems possible to conclude that every historical narrative has as its latent or manifest purpose the desire to moralize the events of which it treats" (1980, 18).

The transition isolated here underlines one of the historical methods of the film: to produce a knowledge of historical relationships by contrasting moments in time, by carving up the time of the story so as to reveal the "inner historicity" of the period rather than simply its outward chronology. Although the use of the flashback structure may seem rather ordinary here, it is an unusual figure in the historical film, and it has far-ranging consequences for the overall shaping of the historical text. The use of an anterior temporal modality enables the film to stage the central event twice—the scene depicting the Day of Liberation is repeated again at the end of the film—inscribing a kind of cyclical pattern into the film's overall historical scheme. (Repetition, as a figure belonging to Genette's category of frequency, will be discussed fully below).

Duration

The category of duration embraces the figures of scene, descriptive pause, summary, and ellipsis. The latter two are especially important in the historical film, enabling it to compress vast stretches of time. The importance of the ellipsis, moreover, goes well beyond the dimension of variations in speed or rhythm — the usual characterization of duration: it serves as a particularly emphatic figure of historical argument, expressing historical relationships according to a distinct cause and effect logic.

In many ways, the ellipsis is the obverse of the analepsis, even though it belongs to the category of duration, rather than order; unlike the seldom used prolepsis, or flashforward — which is usually paired with the flashback — the ellipsis is often systematically employed to render the same kind of causal relationships associated with the analepsis. Like the analepsis, the ellipsis is a "strong" figure of temporality: both involve dramatic leaps in time — one backward, the other forward. In both cases, a cause and effect coding of the temporal relationship is conveyed, with the flashback characteristically unfolding as a kind of "search for the cause" (although this is sometimes made complex, as in *The Last Emperor*), while the ellipsis typically registers the effect of an action in the form of an immediate consequence. By flashing back to the cause, by jumping ahead to the consequence, the historical film is vested with the potential to illuminate and clarify the underlying patterns of history.

The ellipses in *1900* manifest these qualities of historical argument in an emphatic way. In directly juxtaposing two different moments in history, the film introduces a cause and effect logic that brings the discursive nature of the historical project to the forefront; expressing a causal relationship that takes precedence over historical time. While cause and effect logic is characteristic of narrative in general, the ellipsis intensifies the logic of narrative consecutiveness. In the historical film, the refiguration of time in the ellipsis becomes identified with the deep structure of history itself — its logic — which has suddenly been made visible at the level of story, in the conjoining of significant moments. It is as if the secret currents of historical cause were suddenly lifted to the surface and displayed in the diegesis.

There is no fixed convention for the ellipsis in the cinema, other than the hackneyed ones of turning calendar pages or whirling autumn leaves

113

but, like the analepsis, it is abundantly signaled. Two scenes from *1900* will illustrate the way the ellipsis functions in the film. In both, the moment of the ellipse is emphasized by the text, set off so as to highlight its dramatic quality. It occurs, in both scenes, in the middle of a long-take shot, with no disturbance or cleavage in the discourse. The first ellipsis bridges the opening day of the flashback — the birthday of Olmo and Alfredo — to a day approximately ten years later. Here, the idea of time's passage is rendered through the visual trope of camera movement. The camera tracks away from the two patriarchs — peasant and bourgeois — celebrating the births of their grandchildren to frame a row of field-workers, scythes in hand. It then tilts upward to focus on an azure sky. After a few moments, the sky changes color, becoming a bit yellowed. The camera then begins to descend, revealing the same patch of earth now being worked by a red mechanical reaper or threshing machine. Following in the wake of the thresher are the newly dispossessed field-workers; we also see the youthful future Padrone, Alfredo, in knickers and a tie. The ten-year period spanned by this long-take is conveyed doubly: through an immediate historical reference — mechanization — and by the chronology implied in Alfredo's growth.

Here two distinct and important modes of historical argument are encapsulated in the temporal transit covered by the figure of the ellipsis — the relation of cause and effect and the relation of the part to the whole. The passing of the old order and the advent of the new is signified both in the conversion to mechanization and in the growth of a new generation. The births of the two boys are linked to both changes, identified with the initiation of the future, the twentieth century. In addition, part is linked to whole, the particular to the general, through the same figure of ellipsis. The dual births, taken in isolation, represent a particular, local event that happens to occur at the beginning of the twentieth century. The conjunction of the two births with the modernization of the estate, however, clearly inscribes this small-scale, domestic event in an overall historical context. Hence the juxtaposition of these incidents conveys two messages: not only will the two boys preside over a changed world, they will be, to a large extent, agents of change. Not only will they be swept up in the transformation of social and natural life, they will epitomize this transformation.

The second ellipsis I have chosen to exemplify modes of historical argument also draws a heightened significance from the abrupt compression of time. The scene depicts Olmo's departure from the estate, as a young boy, to attend a distant school. As the train leaves the station, filled with youths, the camera focuses on the passing landscape. Then, as the train enters a tunnel, the image is darkened as we watch one of the children's guardians light a cigarette. When the train emerges from the tunnel, the ragged boys on board have been transformed into uniformed soldiers, returning from the war. Here, however, the historical order — the period of the First World War — is invoked without being represented, conveyed without being dramatized.

Olmo's return on the train in the uniform of a soldier carries the weight of representing the entire historical conflict that has been elided in the film, clearly functioning to equate the part and the whole. But, more importantly, this rather surprising elision exposes the underlying discursive project of the film. Unlike in the earlier example, here Bertolucci juxtaposes the two moments in time not so much in order to render a cause and effect logic, but in order to construct a temporal relationship that will express the perspective the film imposes on the past. Bertolucci seems to wish to rescue history from pure spectacle here, to introduce a logic that is lacunar and metaphoric. Lost in the lacuna of the ellipsis is the whole external history of the war. Preserved in the text and sheltered from loss, however, is the historical project of the peasantry, which is maintained with an unwavering focus.

The genealogical project of the film is made manifest in this scene. Bertolucci seems to argue that the war, despite its historical importance, is in fact largely irrelevant to the ongoing struggle between the landowners and the peasants. Despite its "scenic" value, it is inconsequential to this larger struggle and thus left out of the history the film wishes to present. Olmo's education, and the peasant cause itself, may have been delayed by the war, but the political process will continue, a point emphasized by the dramatic elision of the ten or so years in which this struggle was submerged. This is a "willing backward" of the most emphatic kind, a shift in accent or focus that allows a kind of alternative history to come into view, one that speaks to the political commitment of the peasants rather than to the events composing the "official" history of the State.

Frequency

Discussing frequency, Genette explores the relation between the number of times something occurs in the story and the number of times it is represented in the discourse. These relations can be distilled to three types: repeated descriptions of unique events, as in *Rashomon*; single descriptions of repeated events, i.e., the iterative; or a one-to-one relation of event to description, the singulative. In film the repeating form is rarely used and thus clearly stands out; but it is sometimes difficult to distinguish the iterative — single description for multiple occurrences — from the singulative. For example, a scene representing a typical daily dinner, which is meant to stand for a series of such dinners, might suddenly prove to be the occasion of a unique occurrence. The peasant dinner in *1900* illustrates the point: a typical collective repast is interrupted by the symbolic initiation of Olmo into the clan. Genette acknowledges this indeterminacy by devising different classes of the iterative, including the "pseudo-iterative," in which certain events will clearly mark the seemingly commonplace moment as out of the ordinary, unable to be duplicated.

In film generally, the question of the iterative is complicated, for the vividness of detail characteristic of the medium, its concrete expression of the unique texture of every moment, makes it difficult to achieve the quality of generalization essential to the iterative.

1900 is composed of a striking mix of all three types of frequency. The pastoral sequences, on the one hand, convey an image of timeless repetition, of long custom and familiarity with the work in the fields and in the domicile. These scenes are rendered in the iterative mode, which here, as in Proust, is used to signify a certain "freedom from the ravages of time" (Henderson 1983, 34). The film, moreover, seems to avoid, or to deemphasize, the singular occurrences that do take place in the domain of the peasantry. For example, the death of Anita, Olmo's wife — a unique and even momentous event — is not marked or witnessed in any way by the text: it is represented only in a short dialogue sequence, as if it were not consequential in the overall scheme of things. The death of the peasant patriarch earlier in the film is also underplayed, rendered in a way that frees it of the connotations of finitude and closure. The sequences involving the bourgeoisie, on the other hand, constantly show the iterative being invaded by the singulative — with death, marriage, and separation in Alfredo's life made very prominent.

The emphasis accorded these singular events in the domain of the bourgeoisie would seem to tie the bourgeoisie to the historical axis in general, far more so than the peasants with their ongoing but almost changeless existence. But instead, the most decisive historical events of the film are rendered in a temporal rhetoric associated with the peasants. This rhetoric converts the historical process from a series of one-time events to a continuing pattern. The entry into the historical order by the peasants is not registered as a kind of "fall into time," a loss of the timeless world, but instead as part of an ongoing process. The iterative mode of the pastoral scenes is retained by the text for the historical sequences in order to render a type of nonlinear history.

116

The new historical order associated with the cause of the peasantry is represented through a combination of iterative and repetitive modes. For example, the singular moment of triumph in 1945 is rendered twice in the film, at the beginning and at the end. The repetition of the action in the discourse changes the status of the event in the story, transforming the revolutionary moment from a single occurrence to an ongoing series. Although the singulative nature of the event is underlined both times by title cards that announce the precise date and place, the doubling of the scene conveys a cyclicity, as of an event destined to be repeated.

A second example can be found in the scene of the peasant strike of 1919. Clearly a singular event, it is rendered in a manner that makes it appear to be a universal occurrence. The scene unfolds with a certain lack of facticity; there is no title card, for example, announcing the date or the importance of the strike. It obtains a degree of generalization, as if it represented a typical occurrence, instead of a historical event. The music that accompanies this dramatic scene, in which the peasant women lie down in front of the charging cavalry, augments its generalizing quality, as does the choreographed camera work and the dialogue; it signifies its historical status through operatic intensification rather than through facticity.

Repetition, cyclicity, recurrence — these figures of time are highly unusual in the historical film: indeed, they are ordinarily considered to be directly opposed to the "time of history." As Julia Kristeva writes in a different context, history is conventionally associated with a linear conception of time: "time as project, teleology, linear and prospective unfolding; time as departure, progression, and arrival — in other words, the time of history" (1981, 17). To this linear, teleological time, she contrasts the "anterior temporal modalities," which she associates with a different order of discourse: "there are cycles, gestation, the eternal recurrence of a biological rhythm which conforms to that of nature . . . this repetition . . . [is] found to be the fundamental, if not the sole, conception of time in numerous civilizations and experiences" (1981, 17).

The unusual nature of the historical project in *1900* emerges most clearly in its temporal patterning. The time of repetition and the time of history, although seemingly opposed, are interwoven in the film. What is most important is the manner in which the political orientation of the film is associated with the cyclical rhythms of recurrence. The refashioning of historical time as the time of recurrence should not be seen, however, as simply a poetic figuration: it is rather a refusal to view the past retrospectively, a refusal to set the moment of struggle, the moment for effecting change, solely in the past. Above all, what is signified in this deviation from conventional narrative order is an ending that is not a closure. As Bertolucci says: "at that point the action no longer takes place on April 25, 1945 — it's in the present and in the future . . . The proposal made in that episode [the Day of Liberation] steps out of any historic context and that moment represents, for me, the real thrust of the film" (1983, 146). The particular use of analepsis and ellipsis, combined with the striking use of iterative discourse for singulative moments, constitute the boldest features of the film's complex system of tense, a system that permits a very fluid transfer between past, present, and future.

CHAPTER FIVE

Narrative Mood or Focalization

The concept of narrative mood, or focalization, as set forth by Genette, allows us to describe an important partition in the narrative structure of *1900*. While the stress at the level of plot functions, or narrative syntax, is equally distributed between the peasantry and the bourgeoisie, and while the relations of tense are organized to favor the peasantry, the focalization of the film is slanted to the bourgeoisie. The bourgeoisie commands the perspective, the angle from which events are perceived, throughout much of the film. In many ways, the bourgeoisie becomes the narrative "center of interest" when this level of the text is analyzed. It is the bourgeoisie that serves as our "witness" to the years of Fascist terror and to the rise of the peasant class. Furthermore, it is the bourgeois characters who become individuated, psychologically defined, through this focalizing emphasis, in contrast to the peasants, who are defined, for the most part, simply as members of a class.

Focalization can be broadly described as the narrative viewpoint embodied within the world of the fiction, "the different points of view from which the life or the action is looked at" (Genette 1977, 161). Usually a character or several characters will serve as our lens onto the fictional world, but the focalizer need not be human. It is a category separate from both the narrator and the character, operating between them to provide a hinge between narrative "voice" and the diegetic world of the characters. It is one of the most important means of structuring narrative discourse and one of the most powerful mechanisms for audience manipulation.

Although Mieke Bal associates focalization with the question of "who sees" as opposed to the (narratorial) agent "who speaks," this definition has been considerably broadened in recent theory. More generally, focalization defines the center of interest of a particular scene and provides an orientation to it. It can include both the optical and acoustic points of view, although these are not essential ingredients, and serves to communicate a character's emotional or psychological attitude to or perspective on the scene. Recently, Seymour Chatman has proposed new terminology for this function, one that avoids the specifically optical connotations of focalization and point of view alike. The character or characters who observe from a post within the fictional world may assume a special role as screen, reflector, or "filter" of the fictional events and the other characters (1986a). This can be seen as a delegation of the narrator's authority: the narrator may elect to represent all or part of the story from or through a particular character's consciousness or perceptions. Chatman's use of the term "filter" does provide advantages, it seems to me, over the currently dominant term "focalizer," for it expresses well the sense of narrative information flowing through the emotional or psychological channel provided by the character without insisting upon an actual visual outpost. With this refinement, the emotional filter of a particular scene may be understood as separate from the concrete viewing position; the 'screen' or 'reflector' of events may be conceived independently from the literal point of view.

Shlomith Rimmon-Kenan argues for a similar expansion but retains the term "focalization." Like Chatman, however, she finds that the functions covered by this term go well beyond the visual. She subdivides focalization into different "facets," including the cognitive, the emotional, and the ideological focus of the text (1983, 71). I have found that in order to determine the center of interest in many of the scenes in *1900*, it is necessary to invoke at least two of these facets. Accordingly, I will employ the term focalization in Rimmon-Kenan's expanded sense, for its subdivisions lend themselves to close textual analysis. Nevertheless, I am fully in agreement with Chatman concerning the unfortunate tendency to associate focalization with the strictly optical point of view. But where Chatman's term filter gains in generalizing its meaning, it loses the specificity that can be captured in Rimmon-Kenan's model, a specificity necessary for the analysis of this level of *1900*.

In addition to different facets of focalization, there are degrees of consistency and "distance" that should be considered when discussing this category. Bal and Genette, basing their model on the strictly optical definition of the term, distinguish between internal and external focalization. Internal focalization can be bound to a single character or split between two or several characters. When it is split between two characters, it is called variable; when it is divided among several characters, it is called multiple focalization. External focalization, on the other hand, is not tied to a character's perceptions, emotions, or cognition: "an anonymous agent, situated outside the fabula, [can function] as focalizer" (Bal 1985, 105). External focalization, however, is in many ways identical to the function of the narrating agent. Rimmon-Kenan questions the usefulness of this category, and Chatman rather thoroughly discredits it. It appears to be a consequence of Bal's strictly optical sense of the term, and of her insistence that every narrative event is focalized in this strict optical fashion. If Bal cannot locate the "angle of vision" in a character, then she must utilize a category — external focalization — that can account for the "source" of the perception independent of the character. The recent expansion of the functions covered by the term, however, in Rimmon-Kenan's sense or in Chatman's, obviates the need for this category of external focalization, for focalization can now be freed of its rigidly optical meaning and can be understood more in terms of a psychological or cognitive "bottleneck" through which narrative information is transmitted. Hence if a visual source or angle of vision cannot be assigned to one of the characters, one can still speak of the psychological facet, provided there is some kind of characterological consciousness accenting or coloring the scene. Moreover, certain scenes may simply be free of a focalizing or filtering agent, an idea Bal cannot accept, since for her events are always "seen" from a certain position, identifying focalization, as she does, with visual activity. For these reasons, I employ only the internal varieties of focalization in this analysis.

In the opening moments of *1900*, the focalization can be described as multiple. The film no sooner presents us with a peasant character, in the person of a boy singing as he walks through the woods, than it gives us a perspective that overrides the boy's point of view. Within the first few shots of the film, he is ambushed in the forest and murdered. As spectators, we are immediately wrenched from our first site of identification. As the camera hovers over the dying boy, a forceful disjunction occurs between the ostensible "subject" of the sequence — the joyful return to a pastoral existence signified by the singing peasant — and the film's perspective in rendering it.

The focalization from the outset is thus set at a certain emotional and optical "distance" from the protagonists of the day of liberation, almost as if the text is signaling its intention to refuse the spectator the comfort of identifying wholly with a character or filter whose perceptual, psychological, and ideological orientation can be assumed to be "politically correct." Instead, this level of the text will be aligned, for the most part, with the Agents opposing the peasants.

The focalization in *1900* seems to be deliberately askew in relation to the political orientation of the film. Stressing through its concentration on Alfredo, Attila, and Ada the dominant social classes, this register of the text gives the bourgeoisie and the Fascists a prominence that belies the overall message of the film. At almost every key instance in the developing history of the twentieth century, the film observes the event from what is, in many cases, the literal point of view of the bourgeoisie. Where a strictly optical point of view cannot be established, the psychological facet of focalization orients the sequence around the impact the event will have on the bourgeoisie. The bourgeoisie provides the selective perspective from which events, for the most part, are presented.

This may represent a kind of "dialectical" approach on the part of the filmmaker, introducing a different class perspective on events, and also acknowledging his own class position as a member of the bourgeoisie. It might also be read as a reminder to the spectator of his or her own potential for a kind of complicitous relations with the forces in power. I will address these issues more fully in the concluding pages of this chapter.

As the opening sequence continues, the movement to a specific character as internal focalizer is further delayed, almost as if the text were deliberating before assigning this role. Another partisan boy appears in the sequence and appears at first to be designated as the focalizer. He grabs a rifle, exclaiming, "I want to kill, too!" and makes off on his own to the house of the Padrone. He pauses, however, at the door, to wipe his feet clean of mud before entering the villa, rifle in hand, in order to overthrow the centuries-old regime.

Here the focalization is internal, and all three facets — perceptual, psychological, and ideological, appear to reside with the partisan boy. When we do not literally "look through his eyes," he is continually centered in the frame; the character is quite clearly the filter or reflector of the scene. But after the rifle of the boy accidentally goes off, the film cuts away to a close-up of Anita, Olmo's daughter, standing atop a haywagon in order to visually locate the fleeing Attila and Regina. The ensuing cut to Attila appears to be "motivated" by Anita's reconnaissance, but it produces a rather surprising effect. The first shot of Attila is a close-up, showing him casting a loving, concerned look toward his wife, Regina. The remainder of this part of the narrative action consists of the pursuit and punishment of Attila and Regina, with the shots optically divided between Attila and the peasant women. Despite the optical balance maintained between the two sets of characters, the psychological focus has here shifted to Attila, who has been individuated through close-up and point of view cutting, and whose suffering commands, at this point in the film, a measure of sympathy from the audience.

The psychological facet of focalization centers our emotional interest on the character of Attila. At this moment in the narrative, the spectator can clearly "read" the character's emotion of fright and, moreover, can identify clearly the concern Attila shows for his wife. The peasants, on the other hand, are somewhat less individuated during the chase and capture. Multiple focalization has resulted in a split between the peasant boy in the villa and Attila as two "vessels of consciousness" in the opening scenes.

Immediately after Attila is skewered with a pitchfork, the film cuts back to the boy and his captive, the Padrone. A similar shift occurs here. While the perceptual aspect of focalization is divided evenly between the Padrone and the partisan boy, the psychological facet rests with the Patient rather than the Agent of the action. The Padrone's enfeebled aspect, his weary resignation and obvious harmlessness is emphasized. These qualities make him the clear emotional center of the scene.

The third facet of focalization, which Rimmon-Kenan calls the ideological, is described as "the norms of the text . . . the general system of viewing the world conceptually, in accordance with which the events and the characters of the story are evaluated" (1983, 81). The ideological facet of focalization is, in Rimmon-Kenan's system, usually tied to the principal, dominant perspective of the external focalizer. Sometimes, however, a variety of ideological perspectives will emerge. This seems to be the case with 1900, which presents a conflict between these three facets — the perceptual, the psychological, and the ideological. This discrepancy produces multiple perspectives within any given scene, creating what might be called a polyphonic text, wherein different, competing voices make the assignment of a simple, unitary ideological position impossible.

In my view, however, Rimmon-Kenan's notion of ideological focalization should be abandoned, for it embraces a function that can properly be assigned only to a narrator. The focalizer is always subordinate to the narrator in the hierarchy of fictional roles. The narrator may well assign an ideological point of view to the focalizer, but this point of view is always subject to the verification or repudiation of the narrator. The "norms of the text" cannot be assumed to reside with a focalizer, who is by definition a part of the fictional world, for the norms of the text are controlled from without, by a superior, external agency. The problem with assigning an ideological facet of focalization to a character-focalizer is precisely demonstrated in 1900, for the dominant focalizing capacity resides with the bourgeoisie, who could not be said to control the ideological norms of the text. Another argument against this category is illustrated by a different Bertolucci film, *The Conformist*, in which the focalizer, Marcello, is in every way the narrative center of interest, controlling the optical, acoustic, memorial, and psychological point of view. Nevertheless, the character of Marcello is severely criticized in the film: his values, his Fascist beliefs, his cowardice—all are held up to negative judgment. In short, the focalizer cannot control the ideological norms of the text, for to do so would imply a power greater than that of the narrator. In fact, the reverse is the case; the focalizer is subject to the higher predication authority of the external narrator, who frequently repudiates the views expressed or associated with the dominant characters in the fictional world.

In the next major sequence of the film, the births of Olmo and Alfredo, the emphasis again falls on the bourgeoisie. Olmo's birth into the peasant Dalco clan is very briefly sketched and is employed, in a sense, mainly to lend urgency and importance to the birth of Alfredo, who is "lagging behind" in his coming into the world. Here the bourgeois Berlinghieri family receives a detailed expository treatment, with the entire family structure, its internal hierarchies and disputes, its culture and its wealth, placed in the foreground. The perceptual and psychological focus falls on the bourgeoisie, and there is a conspicuous lack of intercutting between the two births. The scene is focalized through the elder patriarch of the Berlinghieri family as he suffers through the birth of his grandson. As the film progresses in this early, expository set of scenes, Alfredo Berlinghieri the elder will receive a great measure of attention, serving as a center of interest equal to that of the two boys, Olmo and Alfredo.

It is with the historical scenes, which inevitably feature a clash between the two classes, that the problem of split perspectives or disparate focal points again emerges. During the great strike of 1919, for example, the perceptual level of focalization is rather evenly divided: the film crosscuts and shifts by way of camera movement from one party in the polemical confrontation to the other. The perspective changes from the bourgeois characters in their hunting boats, to the army, to the massing strikers. Initially, however, the perceptual level of focalization seems to carry less weight than the psychological facet, which clearly favors the peasants. Their cause is depicted as a heroic one: it is their bravery that commands the center of narrative interest.

But an interesting pattern emerges when we regard the perceptual level more closely. The scene begins and ends with the optical point of view of the bourgeoisie. The initial shots of the sequence depict the hunters in their boats, gliding on the river. The closing shots are again taken from the optical point of view of the aristocrats, as they rail at the successful strikers and begin plotting their next move. The scene is thus bracketed in such a way that the bourgeoisie becomes, according to the standard reading of the preeminence of initial and closing shots, the dominant perceptual focalizer.

This has the effect of registering the event through the bourgeoisie and, moreover, of orienting the subsequent scenes around bourgeois response. The scene immediately following the peasants' successful demonstration features the bourgeoisie in church, forming an alliance with the Fascist party and pledging generous financial support. Reinforcing this preeminent perceptual focalization of the bourgeoisie is the fact that we do not witness the logical parallel — the peasants' preparation for the strike; we see none of their rallies, nor do we witness any stirring calls to revolutionary action. Moreover, we do not observe the positive results of the strike in the lives of the peasants. Even the call to arms that follows the murder of three peasant elders by the Fascists is witnessed from the perspective of the Fascists and the bourgeoisie. Indeed, the film from this point forward concentrates almost exclusively, until its closing moments, on the machinations of the Fascists and the bourgeoisie.

The entire middle section of the film revolves around this alliance. We follow closely the courtship and marriage of Alfredo, see his relations with his uncle, and attend to the rising status of Attila and Regina. Olmo is in many ways a marginal figure in the middle section of the film. The scenes in which he does appear emphasize his political impotence and depict the peasant cause as if it had fallen into desuetude.

By listing the sequence of scenes that comprise the middle section of the film, the unequal treatment of the two class protagonists, Olmo and Alfredo, will be revealed. We will begin directly after the scene of Olmo's beating at the hands of the Fascists. Ada pays a visit to Olmo at home, where she comments on the cozy intimacy of the peasant life. The next scene involves Alfredo and his bourgeois cronies and, later, Alfredo and Ada at home, as she sinks further into drunkenness. The film then cuts to Regina and Attila at home, with Regina inciting Attila to improve their material circumstances. Next, Olmo is depicted in the fields, protesting fiercely but ineffectually the arrest of one of his peasant friends; the scene ends with him weeping in frustration. Alfredo and Ada are then shown in the workers' bar, where they reconcile, deciding to have a child. Next, Attila and Regina are shown on their way to Christmas Mass, standing outside the mansion of a bankrupt member of the aristocracy. Then they are invited in, and they murder the old woman. Ada and Alfredo are next seen in their car, happily driving back to the estate. They come upon the corpse of the old woman, whom Attila has skewered atop the spear points of the wrought-iron fence outside the house. Ada at this point screeches off in the car without Alfredo, who is next seen looking for Ada; he suspects Olmo and visits Olmo's house, accusing him of having an affair with his wife. Here Olmo is portrayed as a resigned family man, with little interest in Alfredo, Ada, or the historical events of the day. Next we see Ada and Alfredo together at the estate, where they reiterate their desire to have a child. The film cuts immediately to Attila and Regina's child — they appear to have several — and we realize that the only intact nuclear family in the film is that of Regina and Attila, who have become a fairly prominent couple over the years.

The sequence I have just described constitutes a summary, with many years compressed to show the "typical" course of events. The sequence largely ignores the life of the peasantry, resulting in a dramatic displacement of the peasantry from the historical stage. Only at the end of this sequence does the peasant cause regain prominence. This occurs after Olmo and his daughter Anita stage a small-scale rebellion by festooning Attila with horse manure. In retaliation, Attila intensifies the persecution of the peasants. Olmo, by now a completely marginal figure in terms of the focus of the film, escapes the wrath of Attila by disappearing entirely from the estate. He remains absent for several years. After Attila has vented his murderous rage by murdering several peasants in a mass execution, the film leaps ahead to the "Day of Liberation," which is initiated by a shot of an elm tree (Olmo's namesake) and the sound of peasant singing coming from behind it.

The second depiction of the events of April 25, 1945, displays little of the ambiguous diversity of focalization that we noticed in the opening sequence (except, however, at the very end). Here the peasants receive the textual emphasis, making them the clear center of narrative interest. The events of this scene — the execution of Attila in a graveyard, the return of Olmo, the trial of the Padrone — are clearly focalized through the peasantry. The use of perceptual focalization — with the peasantry providing the angle of vision — combines with a forceful emotional alignment to articulate unambiguously the rectitude of the peasant cause. The text restricts the viewing position and the knowledge of occurrences to that which is perceived and known by the peasants.

This has a curious and striking impact on a scene that has become the focus of considerable controversy in criticism of the film: Olmo's surrender of his rifle to the coalition government that immediately replaces the deposed Fascist regime. The historical "betrayal" of the Communist cause by the coalition of Socialist and Christian parties, the *Committato di Liberazione Nazionale*, seems to be anticipated here. The question that

The scene where Olmo surrenders his rifle to the coalition government has become the focus of controversy in the critical response to the film. At this point Alfredo, whose life has been spared by Olmo's abstract reasoning, delivers the final, cutting words of the film: "The Padrone lives!" to the partisan youth whose declaration "There are no more masters!" inaugurated the body of the film. As Bertolucci says, however: "The film doesn't make a judgment. I think the originality of the film in respect to other political films with historical subjects is that it doesn't judge Olmo." (1990 Copyright © 1976 PEA Produzioni Europee Associate-Rome. All Rights Reserved. Courtesy of Paramount Pictures.)

has perplexed many critics is precisely how this scene should be read. Olmo willingly, even enthusiastically, cedes authority to these new representatives of the State. It is then that Alfredo, whose life has been preserved by Olmo's abstract reasoning, delivers the final cutting words of the film, "The Padrone lives!" to the partisan youth whose declaration, "There are no more masters!" inaugurated the body of the film. Given the absence of external narrative voice in this scene, it is difficult to assess the ideological thrust of the sequence to determine what the final attitude of the film toward the historical coalition of forces in 1945 might be.

But the restricted, character-centered focalization I have described is in fact crucial to the ultimate message of the film as Bertolucci describes it: "The film doesn't make a judgment. I think the originality of the film in respect to other political films with historical subjects is that it doesn't judge Olmo. That is, you can read it two ways. But the thing that counts

127

is that April 25 comes tomorrow, not yesterday. It's made like a prophecy, not a chronicle" (1977, 17).

The strategy behind the film's use of focalization now becomes evident. The peasants are, in effect, left to "speak for themselves" without the intervention of a narrator and without the studied splitting of perceptual and psychological facets that had characterized much of the film. The peasants are here given a point of view on the historical process, a point of view that had earlier resided with the bourgeoisie. In short, the film has underscored the peasants' rise to prominence on the historical stage through its manipulation of focalization that here resides completely—in all its facets—with the peasantry for the first time. Moreover, Bertolucci suspends what we might call the level of narratorial inscription (which I will discuss later), to let the focalizing agents emerge on their own. The ending, as Deborah Young points out in her interview with Bertolucci (1977), can be seen as either for or against what Olmo does, for or against the party line.

A secondary issue emerges through the study of focalization as well— the focalizing power of the women characters. In several key scenes, the psychological facet of focalization resides with Anita, Ada, and Regina. Their perspective is associated principally with critical awareness, providing a focus of lucidity and judgment. Anita, for example, is the political beacon in the film, whose judgment of the future is far more astute than Olmo's. It is through her that events of political consequence—the strike and the burning of the peasant schoolhouse—are first registered: only, however, to have her perspective almost immediately enclosed within the larger perspective of the bourgeoisie or the Fascists. And it is her look-alike daughter who stands atop a haywagon at the end of the film proclaiming that she can see the happy resolution of the historical process. The character of Anita serves as the embodiment of political consciousness.

Ada's role is even more pronounced. In a sense, she serves as the conscience of the bourgeoisie. Her point of view is emphasized twice: at the scene of Olmo's beating (her wedding) and at the site of the Christmas Eve murder of the aristocratic woman. Ada represents the point of view of an outsider, someone not attached to or connected with the estate. In contrast to Anita's scenes, however, the scenes in which Ada provides the center of interest are outside the realm of the historical. Her position is preeminently that of a distant witness to history, one who receives her impressions from the margins. As a focalizer, she registers her impressions almost in the fashion of a Greek chorus, underscoring the brutality and the decline of the world she inhabits.

Additional sites of focalization in the text are provided by Regina and

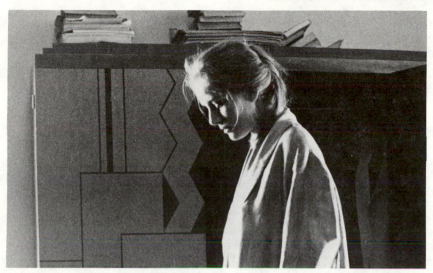

In a sense, Ada's role is to serve as the conscience of the bourgeoisie. She represents the point of view of an outsider, someone not attached to or connected with the estate. The scenes in which Ada provides the center of interest, however, are outside the realm of the historical. Her position is that of a distant witness to history, one who receives her impressions from the margins. She registers her impressions almost in the fashion of a Greek chorus, underscoring the brutality and the decline of the world she inhabits. (1990 Copyright © 1976 PEA Produzioni Europee Associate-Rome. All Rights Reserved. Courtesy of Paramount Pictures.)

Attila, enlarging the film's range of perspectives. The Fascist couple are the primary focalizers in two scenes—the initial alliance of the bourgeoisie and the Fascists and the murder of Patrizio during Ada's wedding to the Padrone. As is the case with Anita and Olmo and Ada and Alfredo, it is the woman of the couple, Regina, who crystallizes the rather inchoate responses and attitudes of her male counterpart. In all three cases, the women characters embody the ideology and emotions informing their class positions in a far more concentrated fashion than the male characters. Anita, for example, is much more political than Olmo; Ada is more critical than Alfredo; and Regina is more malevolent that Attila. A kind of Lady Macbeth, Regina sets Attila on his course and prods him into action, much as Anita does with Olmo.

From this perspective, the male characters appear to be almost passive, less attuned to historical reality than the female characters. One gets the feeling that if the film were set later in the twentieth century, the women would be the principal characters, not just the principal focalizers for several scenes.

129

Reflections on the Model

Two broad patterns have emerged from our study of focalization. Firstly, there seems to be a division of labor between focalizing and acting. While it is the peasantry who "makes history" in terms of the events that are underlined by direct assertions of narrative voice, it is the bourgeoisie who observes and registers its impact. Secondly, in the more intimate sphere of domestic relations, it is the women characters who focalize — and hence clarify in their responses — events of historical consequence, animating and empowering the male characters who ostensibly enact the events of the plot. Thus the film sets its "witnesses" apart from its "actors," but in such a way that the witnesses actually seem to be pulling the strings of the characters who act.

My narrative analysis of *1900* has already revealed several "fault lines," or irregularities, in the way in which different elements of the text fit together. While the Move structure emphasizes the polemical exchanges between the bourgeoisie and the peasantry, the character-system of the text focuses on the two individual actors, Olmo and Attila, who function both as class representatives and as archetypes of nature and history. Moreover, the analysis of focalization discloses that the events of the plot are registered mainly through the point of view and psychology of the bourgeoisie, although the film makes use of some split focalization. Alternating between peasantry and bourgeoisie in the early passages — dividing the angle of vison and the center of narrative interest between the two groups — the middle portion of the film filters the events through the perceptions of the bourgeoisie almost exclusively. The film installs the bourgeoisie as the emphatic center of consciousness through which the depredations of the Fascist period are registered. Thus there is a pronounced disparity between this level and the other narrative structures in the film.

These irregularities do not, however, imply incoherence in the text, nor do they cause difficulty and error in critical analysis. Rather, the skewing of the structures of the text reveals its complexity and its polyphonic character. At each level, a different contradition is posed and a different solution found. A range of messages is projected through these discontinuities that illuminate the several topics of the work — the Marxian class analysis, the archetypal encounter of history and nature, the visionary, Christological current in the film's historical project, the role played by Fascism, the ebb and flow of power, the detailing of a decline of a class. These subjects are interwoven throughout the film in a continuous fashion. They achieve expression through the varied emphases of the different levels of the work, allowing all the messages to resonate at once.

The question of how the film holds its diverse messages together is thus of paramount importance, given the heterogeneity of its structure. Exemplary in its dialogical form and in the compression of its meanings, the text is nevertheless characterized by a controlled play of messages within an overall aesthetic unity. Because of this quality of overall cohesion, the expressiveness of the separate levels of the text is heightened rather than canceled by the juxtaposition of seemingly inconsistent perspectives, just as the Mona Lisa gains by the two different backgrounds on either side of the figure, or as, to use a contemporary analogy, Cubism gains by controlled and incremental shifts of perspective within the overall, two-dimensional unity of the canvas.

In *1900* it is the level of narratorial inscription that controls the formal design of the film and that knits the separate messages into a coherent ensemble. The use of parallel editing and the moving camera are especially emphatic narratorial or "enunciative" devices that clearly impose an overall pattern on the text. In the following section, I will concentrate on these two textual figures as elements of narratorial inscription in order to disclose the way the text binds its messages to the reticule of form.

CHAPTER SIX

Narrative "Voice": Parallel Editing
and the Moving Camera

Theoretical Issues

The complex lamination of different perspectives in 1900 is ultimately related to one of the most troublesome areas of narrative film theory: the question of the cinematic narrator. In the analysis of literary works, the narrator is generally accorded the power to predicate the events of the fictional world, to endorse or repudiate the views and opinions of different characters, to affirm that the incidents described actually occurred: "Every narrative text whose narrator is not hallucinating presupposes a level where a speaker tells a story as true fact and not as invention" (Ryan 1981, 524). These characteristics would clearly be of great value in analyzing and determining the overall "message" of 1900, with its competing points of view and its seemingly contradictory emphases. Standing at the top of the "pyramid of narration," such a narrator would establish the "truth" of the fictional world and, moreover, provide commentary or argument concerning the fictional world, taking on the authority of giving the true account of what really happened, the authority to encapsulate and unify all of the diverse messages that have emerged at different levels of the narrative artifact.

But the significance of designating an external or impersonal cinematic narrator is a question that has been highly contested in recent film theory and that has proven extraordinarily difficult to resolve. Before reviewing this debate, it may be helpful to define more closely the type of narrative activity I am concerned with. There are two basic ways in which a narrator may operate in the film-text: as the personified character-narrator, who tells a story from within the frame of the fictional world — in Genette's terms, the homodiegetic narrator — or as the impersonal or external narrator — the heterodiegetic narrator — who manifests him-/or herself through a range of cinematic codes, including voice-over, but more importantly, I will argue, through camera work and editing. While the internal character-narrator is a concept that can be fairly easily accommodated to existing theories of narration, the impersonal cinematic narration rendered through the camera or other cinematic codes is a considerably more ambiguous area of inquiry. In this chapter I am concerned only with the impersonal narrator, the "instance of emission," and not with the relatively clear-cut issue of the personal character-narrator.

Many critics have argued against the existence of such an external cinematic narrator. The differences among theorists regarding this central question run very deep. Many investigators have concluded that the architecture of narrative form differs considerably when the text is conveyed in a visual rather than a verbal medium. Until recently, this distinction was thought to be reducible to a simple opposition between "showing" and "telling," with the central argument revolving around whether this necessitated a different narrative model or not. Arguing that the verbal model that subtends the concept of the narrator is inappropriate in film, writers such as David Bordwell, Edward Branigan, and George Wilson maintain that the importance of designating an instance of emission in film is minimal. These writers adopt a version of the "non-narrator" theory of narrative fiction. Because nothing akin to a human presence or a speaking subject can be discerned as the source of many narratives, both filmic and literary, it is easier to assume that "nobody speaks," or that the events simply "tell themselves."

Other theorists, however, such as Seymour Chatman, André Gaudreault, and Francesco Casetti, believe that the concept of the narrator is a requirement for any narrative text, including film. According to these writers, the presence of a narrator, whether manifest or implicit, is necessary to conceptualize the architecture of narrative form, providing the governing principle of such elements as the hierarchy of narrative roles, the predicative authority whereby one version of events can be tested against another, and the shaping power to control and vary temporality, thus inscribing a kind of guided reading, a "time of reflection" laid over the "unipunctual" immediacy of the individual shot. Only the agency of a narrator gives us the sense of a true narrative past, the sense of a storyworld that existed "earlier" and "elsewhere" whose occurrence in time can be distinguished from the time of the telling, or narrating.

This position is congruent with the view of many theorists of literature, who believe the concept of the narrator is logically necessary in all fiction. Marie-Laure Ryan argues, for example, that narrative discourse does more than simply refer to a fictional world, it also predicates, asserting and affirming the validity of the story-world, or else placing it in doubt. "Resorting to the concept of the narrator is the only way to account for possible discrepancies between fictional discourse and fictional world" (1981, 523). The narrator is vested with the power to establish the "truth" of the fictional world, to install a guiding viewpoint that can endorse or repudiate the views of the fictional characters within the story-world. Rimmon-Kenan also argues for the logical necessity of a narrator: "Even when a narrative text presents passages of pure dialogue, manuscript found in a bottle, or forgotten letters and diaries, there is in addition to the speakers or writers of this discourse a 'higher' narrative authority responsible for 'quoting' the dialogue or 'transcribing' the written records" (1983, 88).

The need for a concept of the narrator in film can be argued on practical grounds as well, especially in works that require an express authentication of the fictional world. The historical film serves as a primary example. In the historical film, as Sorlin writes: "most of the time there exists a narrative voice . . . the main character is occasionally the narrator . . . More frequently, we read a caption, with a date and details concerning the period: speaking, with the authority that history (common knowledge) gives, the narrative voice tells the audience: remember, in that year, something happened" (1980, 53). The historical film thus departs radically from the historical mode of utterance described by Emile Benveniste, which is characterized by an effacement of the marks of narration: "the historical utterance characterizes the narration of past events . . . Events that took place at a certain moment of time are presented without any intervention of the speaker in the narration . . . No one speaks here; the events seem to narrate themselves" (1971, 206–8).

Although these two descriptions seem directly contradictory, this striking divergence of the historical film and the historical mode of utterance in terms of the style of narration can be linked directly to the issue of authentication in the film text. Without having access to any of the devices or restrictions that lend historical prose its distinctive character — such as the exclusion of pronominal markers indicating the originating source of the utterance and the exclusion of certain verb tenses, such as the present, in order to lend a sense of permanence and finality to the description — film moves in the opposite direction from historical prose and supplies a distinctive level of narratorial inscription to lend authority and persuasiveness to its presentation of the past. It would seem, moreover, that Benveniste's description has a limited applicability even to modes

134

of historiographic prose. It appears to conflict quite markedly with the notion of historical narration offered by Hayden White: "In order to qualify as 'historical,' an event must be susceptible to at least two narrations of its occurrence. Unless at least two versions of the same set of events can be imagined, there is no reason for the historian to take upon himself the authority of giving the true account of what really happened" (1987, 20). *1900* possesses a level of narratorial inscription that corresponds to this predicative function, manifesting itself in ways that can be compared to historical commentary or argument.[1]

The difficulties in designating certain aspects of cinematic representation as manifestations of a cinematic narrator are legion. Above all, the assignment of certain elements to a narrator should not atomize the text, according narratorial status only to graphic titles or voice-over, for example. Nor, however, should *every* element of the cinematic ensemble be taken as a property of the cinematic narrator. It is necessary to distinguish between the activity of the narrator and what might be called the mimetic layer of the text. As Gaudreault has argued, film combines both a mimetic and a diegetic type of narration, both "monstration," or "showing forth," and narration in the sense, not of verbal discourse, but of a reflective, guided reading from a temporal position posterior to the actual occurrences.

The aspects associated with monstration are characterized by their immediacy, by the simple presentation of the fictional world as it appears, for example, in a drama presented on the stage. This dramatic, mimetic level of film should not be considered an aspect of narrative voice. One reason is that the mimetic layer of the text lacks the "double temporality" that narration provides — the sense of a true narrative past in which an agent relates a story about events that happened earlier and elsewhere. Monstration, in Gaudreault's view, is constrained to a kind of "unipunctual temporality." The elements associated with narration, on the other hand, involve the inscription of a properly narratorial viewpoint, a varied temporality that distinguishes between the time of the event and the time of its narration.

For Gaudreault, editing is the major code through which the cinematic narrator manifests itself, inscribing a "time of reflection" between the event and its recounting, placing the event before our eyes in a different sequence from the one in which it occurred, introducing a "guided reading" of the occurrence. Now, although I find the concept of a double mode of narration in film — mimetic and diegetic — of great value, I would like to extend the range of manifestations of the cinematic narrator. Not only editing, but other figures of what used to be called "enunciation" can also be likened to narration and can be shown to fulfill the requirement that a secondary, higher level of narrative authority is involved. Without attempting to catalogue all of the possible manifestations of the cinematic narrator—a project that I think is beyond the scope of film narrative theory in its present state of development—I would like to argue for one other textual mechanism or mode of inscription that I believe bears all of the features of narration: the moving camera. In the analysis that follows, I will treat both editing, specifically the subset of parallel editing, and the moving camera as manifestations of cinematic narration.

I will begin with parallel editing. This type of editing has long been associated with the birth of the "narrator system" in film, to borrow the terminology of Tom Gunning. In the Biograph work of D. W. Griffith, parallel editing represented the first decisive break with the cinema of monstration. With its invention, a varied narrative viewpoint—the freedom to represent spatial and temporal relations according to a discursive logic—established itself over the "unipunctuality" and spatial confinement of earlier cinema. In the work of Bertolucci, parallel editing holds a special importance, for it represents a decisive rupture with the general characteristics of his style, which favors long-takes and the moving camera. When parallel editing does appear, it signifies with special force the shaping of an editorial argument or viewpoint.

The message produced by the moving camera in *1900*, I argue next, is not simply the "showing forth" of the event, but rather, the discursive representation of the event in such a way that a kind of commentary or argument emerges. It effectively restructures events in accordance with a higher narrative message—one that emphasizes the web of relationships among classes, parties, and individuals, and that highlights the wide social consequences of single, seemingly discrete actions. Even more importantly, the moving camera conveys a sense of a double temporal frame, allowing the time of the event to be distinguished from the time of narrating: the characteristic, for Gaudreault, that distinguishes narration from monstration. The occurrence and its recounting are both emphasized here. Camera movement in *1900* can be understood precisely as a refiguration of the punctual event; the occurrence is placed at one remove, as in several scenes the camera elicits a sense of temporal distance, of a growing temporal removal, as if to underscore the process of time working, the process of the present sliding into the past, the conversion of the flux of the present into a kind of articulated formal design.

Parallel Editing in *1900*

Given the dual focalization of the film—its two narrative centers embodied in the two classes—the use of parallel editing or cross-cutting would seem to be a "natural" device. Not only would cross-cutting simplify the development of the parallel lines of action, but it would facilitate the forging of a didactic and symbolic argument, providing a form for rendering striking juxtapositions and telling oppositions, significant parallels and dramatic contrasts. Bertolucci, however, has expressed his resolute opposition to just this type of symbolic underlining and is especially adamant about the use of editing to impose an explicit interpretation on the scene: "The moment of imperialism is the editing of the film. This is when one cuts out all that was direct and 'gesticular' in the rushes; this is the moment when the producer takes over. He takes the electrocardiogram of the film and cuts out all the high points, in order to create a flat line. I believe that a film should be 'all there' at the moment of shooting . . . All you can get from editing is a little bit of manipulation" (1971, 39).

This Bazinian argument gives Bertolucci's political cinema an aesthetic basis quite different from the montage aesthetic we have come to associate with a Marxian cinema, from Eisenstein and Vertov to Godard. Indeed, it is evident that Bertolucci's denunciation of editing is really a repudiation of montage and its "imperialistic" guiding or directing of the viewer's response. Although functional editing within the individual scenes in *1900* is kept to a minimum—with the camera frequently moving rather than cutting to a close-up or medium shot—Bertolucci's comments make it clear that the actual target of his objection to editing is precisely a didactic or rhetorical use of the technique, a type of editing whose foremost proponent would be Eisenstein.

Thus the instances in the film where Bertolucci does create an argument or rhetorical point through editing deserve special notice. Two of the central scenes in the film are constructed rhetorically through parallel editing in a way that lends a symbolic and even a causal dimension to their juxtaposition. These are the two murder scenes that occur early in Attila's Fascist reign of terror: the murder of the three peasant elders in the schoolhouse and the killing of the young boy Patrizio, the son of an aristocrat. Both crimes are linked to sexual passion, here coded as a destructive force. While sexuality and eroticism are, in the domain of the peasants and especially in the case of Olmo and Anita, signifiers of positive, regenerative principles, as I will discuss in Chapter 7, sexuality is here associated with perversion and murder. Desire is a pathological force for Attila and Regina, who are almost demonically obsessed with sex. In addition, the domain of the erotic becomes the medium for the expression of the film's political messages. Alfredo's sexuality, while not deviant, is nonetheless defined by his political and class role, which overtakes his libidinal activities and inscribes them in a context of power and exploitation.

The relationship between sexuality and political message in *1900* is primarily communicated through parallel editing. In the first of the two murder scenes, the death of the three peasant elders in the schoolhouse is closely associated with the seduction of Ada by Alfredo. Here the perpetrator of the murder is unclear, so as to allow a larger sense of complicity and guilt to be expressed. It occurs during the dance hall episode in which Ada, the future wife of Alfredo, has initially made a spectacle of herself by claiming that she is blind and therefore cannot see that she is kissing Olmo, not Alfredo. Discovered in her ruse by Anita, Olmo's wife, she compounds the theatrical effect by proclaiming her apologies loudly and profusely. In the middle of her apology, the alarm is sounded that the schoolhouse is on fire. The dance hall is vacated by the peasants, who rush out to try to extinguish the fire. Alfredo now approaches Ada, attempting to embrace her. She moves away, firing questions and statements: "Who are you? You do not know me. What the hell do you want? You are boring." Alfredo roughly tosses her onto a pile of hay, at which point she begins her recitation of her manifestly fictive childhood history. Alfredo becomes more and more aggressive in his handling of Ada. After she says, "I have no brothers and sisters, I can live where I want, I can have anyone I want," the scene cuts to the conflagration at the schoolhouse. Amid the confusion and noise, Bertolucci muffles the soundtrack and superimposes a group shot of the three old men, smiling directly at the camera in a kind of memorial group portrait. The sound of the fire then resumes on the soundtrack and the shot of the old men fades from view. We then cut back to Ada and Alfredo in the hay, at the moment Alfredo penetrates her.

While the conventional association of flames and passion is ironically placed on display here, a much more powerful causal relation is being established. The pleasures of the aristocracy are directly linked to the perils of the peasantry; the consequences of the callous, unconcerned attitude of Ada and Alfredo are emphasized here by the sound of a child in the background idly playing a fiddle. Ada had been criticized earlier in the scene by Anita for her trifling with the peasants—both with Olmo and with the assembled group—in her "blind girl" act. In a parallel fashion, Alfredo had been admonished earlier in the day by Olmo for the corrupting uses he makes of his money, specifically, his "purchase" of a poor, pretty redhead, who has an epileptic seizure as soon as she begins, at

Alfredo's insistence, to have oral sex with him. The notions of corruption and sex, money, exploitation, and deviancy have been circulating throughout the sequence. These elements emerge fully in the parallel established between the immolation of the peasant elders and the aristocrats' rather theatricalized pleasures, which are obtained in the "rough" style of peasant lovemaking in the hay, a further mimicking of peasant life as perceived by the bourgeoisie.

Significantly, the fact that the Fascist Attila has caused the fire is withheld, presumably to assert the complicity of the aristocracy in the Fascists atrocities. Here Ada's earlier acting of the part of a blind girl is given an ironic but truthful twist. She, and the aristocrats in general, will turn a blind eye to the victimization of the peasant class.

The second sequence in which a political message is expressed through parallel editing begins with the wedding of Ada and Alfredo. Here the association of sex and murder, indidual perversion and class persecution, is made manifest. Regina insults Ada in a vulgar fashion for usurping Alfredo, whom she thought to be her promised, rightful mate, with a degree of spleen remarkable even for her. Ada responds by removing her bride's veil and placing it on Regina, telling her how beautiful she looks, "just like a bride." The combination of generosity and irony silences Regina, and she walks down the hall, as if down the aisle, draped in the veil, toward the sound of raucous laughter coming from the outer room. There she meets Attila, lying on a table, who turns to her, saying, "My bride!"

Later, this perverse couple retreat to an attic hideaway, where she remonstrates with Attila in terms that distinctly recall Ada's words to Alfredo in the hayloft: "What are you? You are a coward. Are you a dog that they treat you like this? Then bark! Bite! Do something!" Attila responds with a line that will turn into a leading motif of this sequence: "Never bite the hand that feeds you, as long as you need to be fed." Regina then spots Ada riding on her white charger into the fields; we view her passage through Regina's eyes — galloping across a landscape fretted with bare tree branches. Regina then begins servicing Attila, as he recites a kind of Fascist litany. Directly after, Attila discovers a "spy" in their midst — the young aristocratic boy, Patrizio, who had earlier admired Attila's strength and especially his black gloves. Regina and Attila begin aggressively tossing the boy back and forth as Regina exclaims, "The best man! We have a best man! Have you ever before served in a wedding?"

It is at this point that the parallel editing begins. The scene cuts to an exterior shot of the fields and forests of the estate, as Ada approaches the camera on her white horse. A white net suddenly comes into view; Ada rides directly into it and pulls up short. Olmo appears and calms the

At the wedding of Ada and Alfredo, Ada responds to Regina's insults by removing her bride's veil and placing it on Regina, telling her how beautiful she looks, "just like a bride." Later, as Ada rides in the fields on her white horse, a white net suddenly comes into view, into which she rides. The white net of Olmo's trap is strikingly reminiscent of Ada's white veil, a point reinforced when Olmo tells her that the net is a "trap for brides." The "trap" Ada rides into is symbolically the trap of her marriage, which will begin to degenerate on this very day. (1990 Copyright © PEA Produzioni Europee Associate-Rome. All Rights Reserved. Courtesy of Paramount Pictures.)

horse, while admonishing Ada to keep still, for fear she will rip his net. The white net of Olmo's trap is strikingly reminiscent of Ada's white veil, which she had presented to Regina earlier, a point reinforced when Olmo tells her that the net is a "trap for brides." Now in a playful mood, Ada asks if he has caught many. He replies: "You are the first. And the last."

Ada and Olmo commence an easy, pleasant conversation, dealing with the estate, which now belongs to her and Alfredo, the beauty of nature, the difficulty of capturing thrushes, etc. As they continue talking, moving into the background of the shot, Olmo asks about the food served at the wedding. A worried aristocrat, the father of Patrizio, appears in the foreground, asking, "Have you seen my son?" Ada answers Olmo's question about the food, reciting the menu, which consisted of lobster, salmon mousse, and suckling pig. At this point the father of the missing boy begins to shout: "Patrizio! Patrizio!" with growing apprehension in his voice.

The film then cuts to a close-up of Attila's gloves, and of Patrizio buttoning his trousers. The boy's face is dirty and tear-streaked, and Attila and Regina are still going at it, in a markedly bestial fashion. Attila scoops Patrizio up and says, "You're not going to tell anyone, are you?" He then grabs Patrizio by the legs and begins spinning him around to the sound of Regina's laughter. He continues to spin the boy in ever-widening circles. Suddenly, the camera lens is half covered in blood, as Attila dashes the boy's head against the pillar and walls of the room. The scene culminates with a low-angle shot of Attila, as if from the dead boy's point of view.

The motif that dominates the parallel editing of the scenes is the notion of the two weddings and the two brides, Ada and Regina. The visual repetition of the veil motif underlines the message of the scene: Regina will symbolically become the true bride, and Ada a pretender, as Alfredo will use the occasion of his wedding to soldiify his ties to the Fascist party, enfranchising Attila and Regina as his "watchdogs." In using the wedding to cement his power, Alfredo simultaneously undermines his marriage to Ada. The "trap" Ada rides into is symbolically the trap of her marriage, which will begin to degenerate on this very day. Regina, on the other hand, will from this day forward begin to acquire power and status from Attila's relationship with Alfredo.

The parallel articulation of the "best man" motif extends the imagery of the wedding to the spheres of friendship, betrayal, and political cross-purposes. Conspicuously absent from Alfredo's wedding is Olmo, clearly the unacknowledged "best man," whose role will instead be that of a scapegoat, used by Attila and Alfredo in a fashion that echoes the use Attila and Regina have made of their "best man."

Directly following the murder of Patrizio, we cut to the search being conducted for the boy. As Ada and Olmo approach from their walk in the fields, Alfredo intercepts them with a certain malice in his eye. Alfredo then gives Olmo a kiss on the cheek. Directly after, Patrizio's body is found. Attila immediately accuses Olmo of the murder. Alfredo stands by and allows Olmo to be savagely beaten by the Fascists, although he is well aware that Olmo is innocent. Thus the two "best men" for the two "weddings" become scapegoats, one for the class and personal wrath of Regina and Attila, the other for the jealousy, insecurity, and political cowardice of Alfredo. What emerges is a union of the aristocracy with the Fascist party leading to the betrayal of the peasant class, a consummation quite different from the one ostensibly celebrated in the scene.

The parallel editing in each of these two scenes renders these symbolic messages unambiguously. While the sequences do not explicitly depict events we ordinarily understand as "historical," the paired sequences both link destructive sexuality to the brute assertion of power; the malign force of history, the history "that hurts," to use Jameson's phrase. This symbolic dilation expresses the controlling narrative viewpoint of the film in a direct and unmistakable way. The message that emerges can be assigned only to a higher narrative authority. None of the other "perspectives" in the film would be able to convey this message or to repudiate it. There is a kind of "knowledge" and awareness manifested here that cannot be attributed to the characters, to the focalizer, or to the syntactic ordering of the events themselves. Only an agent "standing at the top of the pyramid of narration" could juxtapose these events in such a way that a metaphor of the historical forces at work here emerges. While this may still be far from the ideational montage of an Eisenstein, the narratorial power to shape an argument and to provide a metaphor for its expression is clearly displayed in Bertolucci's use of parallel editing. Moreover, of the various figures of historical representation in this film, the use of parallel editing provides an exemplary articulation of the central narrative device of linking the micro-history of the individual subject with large-scale political forces.

The Moving Camera

The moving camera in *1900* functions as a distinct mode of narratorial inscription, defining temporal relationships, imposing a discursive logic on spatial organization, and drawing a secondary, symbolic message from plot events. While Bertolucci's use of the moving camera has long been considered a kind of stylistic signature and hence has been linked primarily to authorship, I will make a case for its specific importance in *1900* as an expression of narratorial viewpoint and agency: rather than emphasizing the role of this technique in Bertolucci's overall style, I will stress the narrative function of the moving camera, particularly the role it plays in sanctioning or predicating the political actions of the peasantry.

I would like to distinguish my approach not only from the concerns typically associated with an auteurist study but also from a different narratalogical approach to film that also "brackets" the category of authorship. David Bordwell's recent work on narrative (1985) comprehends stylistic elements — such as the moving camera — as part of the architecture of narrative form, an approach that treats style as an intrinsic part of narrative design rather than as a component of authorship. Style in this model interacts with and "deforms" the level of plot, causal relations, and chronology, complicating and embellishing the more structured and standardized level of the syuzhet. Elements such as the moving camera or parallel editing function, in his view, as a kind of semantic "basting" of the story or plot material, much as the "accent" in verse may disrupt the strict metrical order.

Nevertheless, this stylistic deformation is not held to be the province of a narrator. Discounting the importance of a narratorial instance of emission in film, Bordwell situates style parallel to the syuzhet, parallel to the level of plot, character, and temporality. Functioning in an equal and complementary way, syuzhet and style work together to control, modulate, and structure the narrative information we receive.

Unlike Bordwell, however, I believe style, especially textual figures such as parallel editing and the moving camera, can be attributed to a narratorial agent, and thus should be situated at a higher level of the pyramid of narration than the characters, the plot, and the other elements that make up the syuzhet or the fictional world. Both textual figures — parallel editing and the moving camera — meet the criteria for a narratorial agent as defined in narratology: they both provide a guided reading of the events, assert the overall ideological message meant to be derived from the text, and establish a temporal distance between the time of the event and the time of its narration, permitting a kind of overview to emerge. These textual figures, in my view, not only inflect, modulate, and deform the narrative material, they provide an overall interpretation of it.

Yet the two devices dramatically contrast with one another. Through parallel editing, a series of metaphors are created in *1900*: passion and destruction are equated, as are marriage and betrayal. It is through these metaphors that an overall narrative voice or narratorial inscription asserts unambiguously the "truth value" of the message that has been produced, affirming, with the authority that only a narrator possesses, the significance and value of these comparisons.

The moving camera, in contrast, possesses a different order of narrative authority. Rather than functioning through metaphor, it seems to derive its power from its interaction with characters and events in an expressive setting, from its active presence as an animate participant. As Bertolucci says: "The camera has a dialectical relationship to the actors and is not merely recording the event, but is an invisible participant with its own soul. Sometimes the camera even enters into competition with the actor — while the actor moves, the camera moves independently" (Kolker 1985, 84). What Bertolucci is describing here, unmistakeably, is a narratorial function; the camera is functioning not as a monstrator, simply recording the action, but instead as a producer of discourse, a participant with a voice — a voice expressed through movement. Rather than placing the expressive charge simply on the actor, as in the mimetic or dramatic arts, the moving camera functions as an equal, even a superior, voice. This voice is offered as the collective viewpoint in *1900*, inscribing a sense of collective agency and affirming the ideological message of the film.

This striking use of the moving camera appears initially in the opening credit sequence of the film, where it is associated directly with the peasant cause. The backdrop for the credits is a painting by Pellizza da Volpedo. Called "The Fourth Estate," this enormous painting was done in 1902 in a heroic realist style and depicts a massed group of peasants striding into an open space in the frontal plane of the canvas. Three figures lead the way, two men and a barefoot woman with a child who seems to be pleading with the two male leaders. The shot of the painting begins in extreme close-up, focusing on the face of the central male figure. It then begins a slow zoom backwards, to eventually reveal the whole of the canvas, which includes dozens of men and women whose purposeful gestures communicate a decidedly martial attitude.

The style and subject matter of this painting is, in effect, dramatized and brought to life in the sequence of the peasant strike in *1900*. Kolker goes so far as to say that the style and content of the painting generate the style and content of the film, finding a similarity even in the color scheme, which is predominately green and brown (1985, 79). But he does not discuss the camera movement, an element that adds another dimension to the message communicated by the painting. By employing the moving camera here, Bertolucci assigns a direct narratorial mandate to the moving camera, valorizing it as the equivalent of a narratorial judgment or endorsement. It gives the sense of a true narrative past to the painting; the film, in effect, promises to narrate the story of the canvas, to fill in the motivating causes and to draw the consequences: to continue, that is, to dilate the frame of the painting, as the camera has begun to do, until the entire story comes into view. The narrator, through the moving camera, also establishes a competence to tell the story, by signifying a kind of retrospective knowledge of where events will lead, establishing a distance between the time of the events and the time of their recounting.

The criterion of temporal distance, set forth by Genette and affirmed, in a different way, by Gaudreault as necessary to narratorial agency, is perhaps somewhat difficult to grasp in connection with the moving camera. Prior to examining in detail the scene I will use to illustrate the narratorial technique of *1900*, a few words concerning temporality and the moving camera in the film are in order. To begin, temporal transitions are rendered exclusively by way of camera movement throughout *1900*, as if one scale of movement were geared up to represent the passing of entire decades. At one point, for example, in a transition already discussed under the category of tense, the camera tilts up from one group of peasants and

144

focuses on the sky; it then glides back down to discover the same set of characters, now ten years older. In another example, the camera at the end of the film lifts itself out of the courtyard, where Olmo and Alfredo are scuffling after the "Day of Liberation," to descend into close-up to reveal the same characters, now old men, continuing their shoving match. Once more, a decade or more has been compressed into a scale of movement that can be encompassed by the moving camera, which is the film's most significant marker of temporal change.

The point is that the moving camera is used specifically to signify temporal transitions and temporal processes. In this capacity, it inscribes a kind of narratorial overview, a power to refigure the order of events according to a temporal logic that is not chronological, not part of the story-world per se, but rather is imposed from without, from the vantage of an agent who is reviewing events that have occurred "earlier." The moving camera is vested with the power of temporal figuration, and through this, with a clear-cut range of narratorial powers.

The narratorial agency communicated through the moving camera expresses itself also in sequences that are free of direct temporal manipulation. In the pages that follow, I will analyze one scene as an example of narratorial inscription: the confrontation on the road between the striking peasants and the military. Through a combination of tracking shots, pans, tilts, and movement within the frame, this scene comes to represent not only the clash between different classes but the structuring of a narrative and historical message through movement.

In dramatizing the peasant strike of 1919, the narrator utilizes a complex and varied battery of camera techniques. The scene occurs directly after Olmo's homecoming from the war and explicitly places Anita, Olmo's comrade/wife, at the front of the revolutionary movement. It begins with a shot of a line of soldiers, high on the road, whose horses are startled by the sound of nearby gunfire. The film then cuts to two close-ups of ducks falling into the water, followed by a shot of several small boats with the hunters standing in them moving slowly down the waterway. The initial connection between the landowners and the soldiers is thus established acoustically by the gunshots. Several additional close-ups of dying waterfowl are quickly presented, after which a series of short tracking shots brings the soldiers and the landowners into immediate spatial proximity. The moving camera combined with the montage of dying waterfowl is used to underline the fact that the landowners are the agency behind the imminent military retaliation against the strikers.

The next sequence of shots begins with a long-shot of peasants in heavy-laden carts moving into the foreground. A tracking shot follows that brings Anita into view along with other militant peasant women who are attempting to persuade the fleeing peasants on the cart to stay and fight. As a distant shout is heard, the camera begins what is approximately a 360° pan that encompasses the entire landscape, linking the strikers to the frightened peasants in their carts and ending with a view of the approaching cavalry on another road. We then cut to a medium shot of Anita and the other women and children positioning themselves on the road, the site of the approaching confrontation, and begin to track right in medium close-up to detail their faces.

In this scene the camera is constantly moving, always in the direction initiated by movements within the frame. Lateral tracks right and left are joined directly together, with the centerpiece of this sequence consisting of the circular scan of the landscape. This shot forms a visual contrast or opposition to the centerpiece of the preceding set of shots—the montage close-ups of the dead and dying waterfowl. But the sequences have one attribute in common—the fact that an off-screen sound has motivated the composition of the shots. In the opening shots centered on the landowners, it is gunfire that links the soldiers on the road, the dying waterfowl, and the landowners on the river. In the case of the peasants, the sound of a human voice, calling from across the expanse of landscape, joins the strikers to the fields and the roads and, by implication, to the larger domain of the peasant world. Distinguishing the two sequences, however, is the fact that in the first part, the camera cuts to the separate spaces; in the second, it joins the peasants to the landscape by way of the inclusive imagery of the circular pan.

One of the most striking aspects of this scene is the display of courage shown by the women. Anita directs her entreaties to the peasant women, as if there were a bond between them that could be invoked and relied upon for political struggle. When the two captains of the cavalry give a futile, preliminary order for the women to clear the road, they ride away to disclose behind them a cart occupied by three generations of peasant women. Anita immediately rushes forward to enlist them in the cause. The visual association is unmistakeable: the women here are the equivalent of the frontline soldiers, analogous to the leading officers of the cavalry. This is in sharp opposition to the partriarchal order maintained by the college of Padrones and gives the scene a definite, and contemporary, feminist orientation.

The remainder of the scene revolves around the political effectiveness of the peasant women as leaders of the strike. The camera movement reinforces their centrality. At this point the peasant men seem beset by indecision. As they retreat from the road and tentatively gather sticks to

One of the most striking aspects of this scene is the display of courage shown by the women. As the camera moves along the file of strikers, the women lie down, row by row. The cavalry commences its charge, but draws up just short of the women, refusing to trample them. The scene revolves around the political effectiveness of the women as leaders of the strike, giving the scene a definite, and contemporary, feminist orientation. (1990 Copyright © 1976 PEA Produzioni Europee Associate-Rome. All Rights Reserved. Courtesy of Paramount Pictures.)

be used as clubs, the singing of the peasant women is heard. The women are already massed on the road. The camera now resumes moving, tracking the men as they join the women, tracking the women as they move ahead to the front lines. As the camera moves along the file of strikers, the women lie down, row by row, recalling the test of courage Olmo and Alfredo undertook beneath the train early in the film. We then cut to the Padrone, now out of his boat and walking next to the soldiers. The cavalry commences its charge, but draws up just short of the women, refusing to trample them. As the military retreats, there is a shot of the Padrone and his friend, who shoots a round from his shotgun into the mass of assembled peasants.

The symbolic geometry expressed through camera movement does more than simply present a stylized treatment of a crucial moment in the film: it clearly predicates the event, affirming its importance, highlighting it as an emblematic expression of the film's central message. In this way it is manifestly a narratorial device. But the temporal mode employed here seems to be the unipunctual time of monstration, rather than the dual tem-

147

poral frame of narration: it appears that there is no distance between the time of the event and the time of the recounting—the decisive factor, according to Gaudreault, separating narration from monstration. However, the moving camera generalizes the strike, making it seem less like a punctual occurrence and more like the summary of an ongoing series. And it is in this fashion that the moving camera manipulates temporality in a way that allows us to describe it as a narratorial agent in the strict sense of the term.

The moving camera thus cues a shift in the tense system of the film, invoking a temporality that is not the unipunctual time of monstration. The iterative mode here takes over from the singulative, suggesting a whole history of such occurrences, a continuing series of such confrontations, as I have described in detail in my chapter on tense. The moving camera triggers a switch in temporal codes. Simply by generalizing and aggrandizing the event—amplifying it through sweeping, rhythmic movements—the moving camera fashions a kind of temporal overview that frees the depiction from the rigidly synchronous time of monstration and delivers it to the special "time of history" that the film reserves for its visionary moments.

In short, Gaudreault's limiting of narratorial inscription in film to the temporal control afforded by editing must be expanded to the register of tense in general and to the range of devices that enable film to invoke temporal options other than that of the singulative. We have discussed the ways in which the moving camera can convey a dual temporal frame, providing a time of reflection superimposed over the time of the event, thus allowing for the inscription of a true narrative past. It thus fulfills the most rigorous definition of narratorial agency, predicating the event, affirming its significance by investing it with specific temporal properties. Other types of narratorial inscription may also be discovered in film that fulfill these requirements. Gaudreault's model is the most rigorous and closely argued attempt to come to grips with the difficult double mode of presentation in film. It is, however, extremely restrictive. Without rejecting or revising his model, I have expanded the instances of narratorial inscription in film from the overly limited instance of editing to a more supple approach that recognizes the narratorial powers of the moving camera as well. Above all, we have discovered that the system of tense in film can be invoked by devices other than editing, and that it is in the control of the system of tense that narrative "voice" in film is to be found.

CHAPTER SEVEN

The Somatization of History:
Symbolic Patterning in *1900*

In the preceding analysis I have stressed the way the visual design of *1900* functions as a form of narratorial overview to link the different themes of the work. Through camera movement and parallel editing, unity is imposed on the diverse signals the text projects. In attending to this interplay of messages, symbolic patterns have been revealed that offer additional perspectives on the film. In this chapter, I will address symbolic patterning — understood as imagery that condenses the motifs of the text in a highly metaphoric or associative manner — directly as another type of historical argument. I will focus on the interplay of psychoanalytic and historical modes of representation, which find expression in the concentrated imagery of the body that pervades the film. This level of the text is not accessible to a narratological reading, nor to textual analysis per se, for its logic is associative rather than structural. It operates through the overdetermination of certain key motifs. In this section, the theme of the utopian, a motif that imbues the text throughout, will be brought into relief by privileging the connotative and associative logic of the film. I will also discuss music here as a connotative attribute of the work.

History in *1900* is fashioned much like a gestalt drawing, with two highly antagonistic versions of time and events unfolding within the same narrative space. From one perspective, the film purports to analyze the "poetic awakening" of the Italian peasant class to their own historical significance; from another, it appears to concentrate on what psychoanalysis calls the destiny of the individual subject. As Bertolucci says, "Everything that happens in this film on a personal level is thus relegated to have a larger, historical meaning" (1975, 13). But in spite of this attempt to reconstruct the formation of individual subjectivity as an allegory of a broader history, these two narrative schemas—the imaginary history of the subject and the history of the construction of a revolutionary class—are largely contradictory. With the psychoanalytic subject installed at the center of the historical process, history acquires a predetermined outcome, conforming to a fixed pattern of positions and roles. Moreover, this type of narrative apparatus is capable of registering public events only where they impinge upon the individual character. Subordinating political history to the narrative *telos* of subjectivity, the film seems to willfully evade the material contingencies of historical transformations.

But a contrary and equally compelling argument is that it is precisely the narrative structuration of history in *1900* and its foregrounding of teleology that express its political message most fully. Narrative form, and the teleological orientation intrinsic to it, may be seen as central elements indispensable to a Marxian reading of history. It is through the teleological orientation of narrative form that the identity of the singular moment with the scattered time of history is established. Without a teleological destination, as White comments, "Marxism loses its power to inspire a visionary politics. Take the vision out of Marxism, and all you will have left is a timid historicism of the kind favored by liberals" (1982, 5). What Jameson calls the fear of utopian thinking in current Marxism makes it impossible to imagine a radically different social formation of the future.

It has therefore fallen to the arts, according to White, to rediscover and cultivate this theme. *1900* is a striking case in point: it restores this repressed, "forgotten" theme of Marxism to the forefront, staging an openly wish-fulfilling, utopian resolution to the historical tribulation of the peasantry. Furthermore, its "dream of ideal community" flows directly from the narrative form of the work, which links past, present, and future in a patterned unity. In a surprising reversal of expectation, moreover, the very "romance of the subject," which at first appeared to contradict the wider designs of an authentic class history, now appears to convey the utopian message. Far from deviating from the Marxian topic of the film, the destiny of the individual subject proves to be essential to its articulation, for it is through the Oedipal patterning of the text that history in *1900* becomes invested with desire—a precondition for the emergence of the theme of the utopian. This admixture of history and desire goes well beyond the simple fashioning of maternal and paternal correspondences to the historical process: the utopian register in the film emerges through the kind of somatic drama generally encountered under the rubric of the history of the subject, but here applied to the collective body of the peasantry. In addition, I believe that the articulation of a collective synthesis is dependent upon the kind of fictional patterning that produces and organizes the subject's individual desire. The "dream of totalization" that desire affords on a personal level — "the identity of the one with the many" — is here translated into a model of the historical process. We might say, echoing Jameson, that an older, Oedipal structure in *1900* is emptied of its original content and subverted to the transmission of an entirely different, utopian message.

Desire in this expanded sense thus comprises the principal vector of historical events in *1900*, determining their course. It constitutes what narratology would call a core semantic structure, unifying different narrative actions. Consequently, it not only operates in the service of the utopian theme, but also conveys the destructive, annihilatory forces of history. Both are generated from the same dynamic of plot. Counterposed to the clairvoyant history of the peasants, with its invisible yet structuring domain of the utopian, is the type of history associated with the Fascists, which is manifested in *1900* as sadistic spectacle. The persecutory figure of Attila, for example, the leader of the Fascists, whom Bertolucci calls the "summary concentrate of all the aggressive forces in the film" (1975, 18), clearly represents the inversion of utopian values: yet his very destructiveness shares the eroticism associated with the utopian aspect of the text. What emerges is a pairing familiar from psychoanalysis — a history turned by erotic and destructive forces. The film thus seems to demonstrate that the patterning of history obeys a deeper logic, a deeper classification system, that it is mediated by what Jameson calls the "codes and motifs . . . the *pensée sauvage* of the historical imagination" (1988, 152). The history of class antagonism and the imaginary history of the subject here interpenetrate, unfolding within the unity of a shared code, an unconscious "master plot" of struggle, domination, and rebellion.

The initiatory events of the plot can be read in terms of this dual significance. The quote from Bertolucci describing this scene bears repeating: "It's a day, the 25th of April, the Italian Day of Liberation, and it includes the whole century. We took it as a sort of symbolic day on which is unleashed, on which flowers this peasants' utopia . . . this day of utopia contains the century . . . the premise of this day lies in the past, but the day also contains the future" (1975, 16). What Bertolucci calls the "stratification of time elements," the simultaneous projection of different temporal frames, is thus one of the signifiers of the utopian, as we have seen earlier in the discussion of narrative domains. Most importantly, this simultaneity condenses the historical and the psychoanalytic dimensions of the text. In the opening moments of the film, this theme is expressed through the partisan youth who holds the Padrone captive with a rifle. When the Padrone asks him his name, the boy replies "Olmo." When asked if he knows who Olmo was, the boy partisan says simply, "He was the bravest." The opening images of the film thus immediately intersect two moments in time, skewering the past to the present. The revolution, the text implies, has become young again, while the old regime of the landowners has faded. The effects of temporal processes seem to register only on the body of the Padrone, while the peasant class is seen as perpetually young, perpetually engaged in struggle. The confrontation of the Padrone and the youthful peasant, however, also carries a strong psychoanalytic connotation. Two messages are superimposed in this scene: it represents both the culmination of the historical process — the end of history — with all moments compressed into one, and a rehearsal of the psychoanalytic pattern of Oedipal repetition, the inevitable recycling of generational conflict.

It is through this double narrative *telos* of subjectivity and history, which crystallizes around the image of the body and its subjugation or renewal, that the text projects an alternative history in which the course of empirical events is transformed into the "possible world" of the utopian. History is in effect "somatized" in *1900*, embodied and represented in a way that recalls Marx's observation that even the senses have become theoreticians. At the film's denouement, for example, Olmo's daughter Anita stands atop a haywagon and proclaims that she can see, off in the distance, the routing of all oppression and the restoration of a harmonious world. The libidinal and erotic aspect of the utopian vision she articulates is explicitly rendered here, as the character puts her hands between her widespread legs as she looks off into the distance and joyfully describes the advent of a new age, conspicuously associating desire with a transfigured world. The erotic connotations of the utopian are rendered in an equally explicit fashion in an earlier scene. As Olmo and his pregnant wife make love, the camera focuses on a primitive drawing on the wall behind them featuring a red banner carried aloft to a rising yellow sun. This lamination of images associates revolution with the natural processes of conception and birth, a notion reinforced by the fact that the child here in the womb will grow into the adolescent girl who stands atop the haywagon at the end of the film, legs wide in a gesture of fecund pleasure.

The body itself thus becomes the principal site of the historical conflicts focused by the work, the junction of the utopian and the repressive tendencies implicit in its unfolding. The somatization of history in the film is concretely expressed not only in scenes of erotic interaction, but also in the foregrounding of the body as a figure of collectivity. This takes the form of the psychoanalytic drama of the whole body versus the body in bits and pieces. On the one hand, an emphasis on lost objects, part objects, runs through the film: a missing ear, an absent father, a runaway wife, a stolen pistol. On the other, a sense of a collective body, infinitely extensible, emerges from the utopian message of the text. The conflation of the individual body and the collective body in the domain of the peasantry provides a positive reworking of the somatic crises typically enacted within the Oedipal framework. It is a history, like *Finnegan's Wake*, in which the individual body becomes the projective ground for the unfolding of a national history.

One passage illustrates this opposition quite clearly, commingling the images of the continuous body and the body disaggregate. It begins with Olmo and Alfredo as boys, waiting out a storm in a loft where they cultivate silkworms (a scene reminiscent in setting and imagery of the "silken kimono" sequence in *The Conformist*). Olmo takes off his wet clothes, and the two boys compare penises. Alfredo is circumcised, while Olmo is not, and they remark upon its similarity to the silkworms. When the storm breaks, a radiant city is suddenly made visible on the horizon. As Olmo describes the unfamiliar steeples and smokestacks in terms of ship's masts and tall trees, with Alfredo correcting him, a strong sense of wonder and possibility arises. The scene as a whole suggests a kind of prelapsarian existence, with the individual body, the natural world, and a kind of utopian landscape woven into the same configuration.

This mood is dramatically altered, however, in the ensuing scene. As the two boys run into the fields to tell of their vision of the city, they encounter the Padrone, berating the workers for the damage the storm has caused. Estimating that half the crop has been destroyed, the Padrone decides to cut the workers' share in half. In a gesture of defiance, one of the peasants — a minstrel — takes his knife and cuts off one of his own ears, handing it to the Padrone. The Padrone strides away with the ear firmly clenched in his hand.

This gesture of self-mutilation inscribes the body directly into political discourse. The oppression of an entire class is signified by the maiming of a single body. It is the definitive reversal of the sense of somatic unity established earlier. Olmo's point of view is again emphasized, as his grandfather expressly tries to keep him from witnessing the act, to no avail. Again, the figure of the Padrone explicitly condenses the notions of the punitive father and the class tyrant.

The severed ear in the possession of the Padrone may thus be said to signify the captivity of an entire class. The somatic level at which this class discord is expressed, however, is described by Bertolucci as a prepolitical moment: "It's a very individualistic protest gesture, still, which synthesizes, however, the desperation, the misery of a whole group of peasants, and which in the next scene is immediately carried further as I show how the idea of the strike is born" (1975, 16). The body thus inaugurates a trajectory that leads to the peasants' full embrace of the historical process. The body in pieces becomes an analogue for the enslaved social body, while the aggregate body of the strikers becomes a figure for an ever-widening kind of unity.

Directly after this prepolitical moment of self-mutilation, however, the film invokes the utopian theme that subtends and precedes the overtly political actions of the peasantry. It is signified here by the production of music, which will prove to be the emblematic expression of the utopian throughout the film. After returning to his family, minus an ear and nearly bereft of food for the day, the peasant begins to play a tune on his ocarina. The soothing music seems to be addressed to the missing ear and, beyond that, to the peasants' condition of servitude and loss in general. The association of music with the recovery of a lost plenitude is indicated here and made explicit at the end of the film, when various peasants demand that the Padrone make restitution for their missing fingers, husbands, and teeth. These demands are all followed by musical interludes, as if the peasants were invoking a domain in which injury and deprivation did not exist.

Music is associated throughout the film with moments of political significance. Its function in *1900* can be compared to Jacques Attali's idea of music as a herald of social change, presaging a new social formation in a "prophetic and annunciatory way." In Attali's view, change manifests itself in music before it is reflected in social institutions. Music may thus be interpreted as a prefiguration of future social formations. This is borne out in *1900*. The convulsive transformations of the social order in the twentieth century are literally announced by the death of Verdi, an announcement that introduces the body of the film beginning in 1901. The music of Verdi rises ominously on the soundtrack, together with the lament of the jester Rigoletto that "Verdi is dead!" as a bridge between the Overture and the main part of the work, coupling the ringing statement of the boy partisan in 1945, "There are no more masters!" with the first cries of the newborn Olmo in the year 1901.

One could analyze the "sedimentation" of music styles in the film—the peasant sonorities, the Verdi passages, the minimalist abstractions of Ennio Morricone—as representative of specific social formations co-present in the film. But the only significant *diegetic* music originates with the peasantry. Music in this context is directly related to the theme I have been elaborating here—the individual body as an image of the social body. It serves as an agent of transformation in the film, fulfilling the promise of a social utopia. It thus recodes the agon of the body, which is so prominent a feature of peasant life, into an instrument of political expression.

The two workers' strikes, for example, are strongly marked by music. In the strike of 1908, there is a lone accordionist who follows the departing train that carries Olmo and the other peasant boys off to school, a train decked out in the red banners of the striking peasants. The martial component of the music is escalated in the strike of 1919, as a full-scale chorus issues from the massed strikers. Music is played at the climax of the film as well, especially during the trial of Attila and the Padrone, which takes place in a graveyard (as Attila intones: "I am that cruel time . . ."), and which is literally organized around its musical interludes. And in the film's final sequence, an epilogue featuring Olmo and Alfredo on the day of their deaths, a lone musician is again heard as the film shifts into a new temporal mode of simultaneity in which past, present, and future are compressed into one. In this visualization of the unity of separate instants of time, music comes to replace speech, as if the utopian offered a different mode of communication as well as a different order of time.

Functioning almost as a musical extension of the film itself — like the closing ballet of a Renaissance comedy — the ending of the film represents an explicit staging of the utopian dimension. Here the two antagonists, the now elderly Olmo and Alfredo, are transformed into youthful versions of themselves, as the film cuts between their past and present manifestations. Here, too, the characters have aged so as to become virtual doubles of the grandfathers. Many of the features we have associated with the utopian — the multiplication of temporal frames, the renewal of the body, the presence of music — are manifested in this lyrical coda. The canceling of the negative effects of temporal processes, a theme that had been encoded in the music, emerges here directly.

But there is an inconsistency here as well, which I believe can be resolved only by returning to our original problematic of desire and history. The utopian theme has been associated throughout the film with the peasants. The division between the peasant world, with its structuring domain of the utopian, and the quotidian world of the aristocracy, has been so pronounced — distinguished expressly by the absence of temporal and physical decay in the peasant world — that we may speak of the narrative universe of *1900* as a split narrative world, with very different "systems of regularities" governing each world. Nevertheless, Alfredo, the Padrone who presides over the persecution of the peasantry, is part of the utopian resolution of the text. Bertolucci, indeed, speaks of the two principal characters of *1900* as if they were equivalent: "In the end, I find that these

155

Bertolucci speaks of the two principal characters of *1900* as if they were equivalent:
"In the end, I find that these people are the reverse faces of the same personality, that
each represents one part of a complex character. Thus they are not only representatives
of a dialectic of a social nature, but they can sort of help us to peep into the inner
structures of the century." (1990 Copyright © 1976 PEA Produzioni Europee Associate-
Rome. All Rights Reserved. Courtesy of Paramount Pictures.)

people are the reverse faces of the same personality, that each represents
one part of a complex character. Thus they are not only representatives
of a dialectic of a social nature, but they can sort of help us to peep into
the inner structures of the century" (1975, 15).

The music that accompanies the utopian reunification of the two antagonists at the close of the film reinforces the central message of the body
as a figure of social and historical processes. As Attali writes: "Music, directly transected by desire and drives, has always had but one subject —
the body, which it offers a complete journey through pleasure, with a beginning and an end. A great musical work is always a model of amorous
relations, a model of relations with the other, of eternally recommence-
able exaltation and appeasement, an exceptional figure of represented or
repeated sexual relations . . . Any noise, when two people decide to in-

vest their imaginary and their desire in it, becomes a potential relationship, future order" (1985, 143). The "codes and motifs" of the historical imaginary are thus placed on open display in *1900*. The history of the twentieth century is seen to result from a kind of traumatic splitting, as in psychoanalysis, of an original unity. Thus the somatic expression of history in the film receives its final figuration in an image reminiscent of Plato's androgyne: an emblem of sexual unity and division translated into class terms.

CONCLUSION

In the preceding analysis I have concentrated on the narrative structuration of history in the film-text in order to disclose the deeper patterning, what Jameson calls the "pensée sauvage" of historical reckoning. This main current of my study flows into several neighboring areas of critical inquiry. Each level of the narrative artifact involves problems in narrative theory that have been resolved, I believe, in the direction of maximum explanatory power and in a direction congruent with an "intuitive" understanding of the text. Above all, the resolution of theoretical problems has not taken place in an abstract fashion, with the achieved solutions applied after the fact to the film; rather, the theoretical solution has at every point been checked and conditioned by the text at hand, by the very real encounter with the form and structure of the film.

In this way I have attempted to set up a dialogue between the theoretical discourse and the film itself. While the film has shaped and influenced the theoretical procedures I have chosen to employ, the narrative theories I have adopted have exposed the quite extraordinary complexity of narrative structure in the work. In some ways, the theory has "rewritten" the film, but these ways are, I believe, provocative and enriching and true to the film's own multivalent perspective on the historical process.

What the close analysis of the film's diverse narrative strata has revealed is the layered and discontinuous nature of the artifact. Each level of the text seems to address a different problem of historical representation. Each level, likewise, poses a different solution, involving competing symbolic requirements. At the functional level of plot syntax, for example, the problem of modeling the plot is complicated by the implied chronology of the

158

historical order itself. While the film maintains a fairly straightforward chronological trajectory, the points at which the Move structure deviates from straight chronological order represent decisive transformations in the way history is represented and understood. The Move analysis has shown that the logic of historical cause is more effectively rendered when the plot design is not strictly subordinated to linear temporal succession.

The analysis of the character-system of the text allows other elements of the narrative universe of *1900* to emerge, such as the partitioning of the narrative world between the domain associated with nature and the domain associated with history. It is at the level of the character-system, as well, that the invisible narrative domain of the utopian — a domain that pressures and informs the text at all its levels — can be concretely described and methodologically expressed. But the analysis of the character-system reveals aspects of the text that are in some ways contradictory to the logic of the Move structure, or plot syntax. The character-system is constructed around a central opposition between nature and history, which is embodied anthropomorphically chiefly in the characters of Olmo and Attila. The functional syntax of the plot, on the other hand, relegates these two characters to the role of Auxiliaries, with the cardinal opposition consisting of the contest between the two classes, bourgeoisie and peasantry. While the characters of Olmo and Attila are primary in the analysis of the character-system, wherein they are revealed as Protagonist and Antagonist, Hero and Villain, they are secondary in the analysis of the Move structure, which stresses their lack of direct confrontation. This discrepancy constitutes one of the major fault lines of the text, which reveals the sedimentation of different messages, different generic forms, in the work.

Thus at the functional level, one problem of historical representation is resolved, while at the actantial level another, equally consequential, symbolic resolution is achieved. Moreover, one level seems to address itself to deficiencies in the other. This pattern of diverse solutions that initially seem to contradict one another but ultimately are shown to balance one another, persists throughout the text.

The other major tributary of my analysis is the discourse of historiography proper, which has been increasingly geared to questions of narrative structure in historical writing and to disclosing the narrativist modes of explanation that underpin historical reckoning in various periods. The work of Hayden White, Paul Ricoeur and Fredric Jameson has proven particularly useful in relating the wider currents of historical discourse to the particular narrative theories I have used to analyze *1900*. Armed with the knowledge that historical writing shares many features with narrative fiction, I have proceeded to treat the film as a historical work that employs

159

sophisticated methods of historiographic explanation. My intention has been to disclose the overall theory of history animating the text and to highlight the particular techniques that the film shares with traditional forms of historical analysis. The film goes beyond traditional methods, however, to essay a mode of historical causation that White and Foucault have called genealogical: the seizing of the past not as a fixed and permanent order but as an open form, subject to changes in perspective, containing elements that can be perceived as leading to a future that one wishes to attain, rather than seeing the past as leading ineluctably to a preordained present. It is this genealogical or narratological mode of historical reckoning that the text sets forth as its principal instrument of historical judgment and analysis.

It is in the tense system of the film that this powerful theory of the historical process is asserted most directly. The analysis of tense is, I believe, one of the most illuminating methods of modeling the discursive project, the overall philosophy of history informing the film. It is a technique little utilized in film studies. Certain genres, however, especially the genre of the historical film, can be productively "unfolded" through this type of analysis. The study of tense deals with the ways in which time is carved up into narrative temporality, the ways in which temporality is encoded to disclose symbolic messages about the narrative universe, and the ways in which temporality can serve to articulate the most far-reaching and yet most elusive arguments concerning the historical issues at stake in a particular work. Furthermore, in my analysis of tense, I have come to the conclusion that the control of narrative temporality is one of the most important manifestations of narrative voice in film, and that further inquiry into the problem of narrative voice in film must begin with the power of temporal manipulation vested in the cinematic narrator.

The chief value of my overall analysis lies, I believe, in the demonstration of the efficacy of narratological inquiry for the description and modeling of a film that contains a great range of voices and messages. I have sought to use narrative analysis to bring to light as many of these messages as possible and, furthermore, to show how they are unified in an overall design. Narrative analysis provides a precise and concrete method for revealing the structural properties of a narrative work, the architecture of narrative design, in which the most significant messages about the fictional world inhere.

Finally, the analysis of *1900* has revealed a text criss-crossed by numerous "socio-symbolic messages," to borrow a phrase from Jameson. Each layer of the narrative composition produces a strong signal about the fictional-historical world of the text. The variety of storytelling techniques superimposed in the film speak to the complexity of historical representation; each level can be read as a different way of articulating the events with which the film deals. In combining these perspectives, *1900* offers an approach to the historical past that is exemplary for its openness and multiplicity.

NOTES

Chapter Two: The Structure of the Plot

1. The Move Grammar devised by Pavel addresses one particular problem that has been ignored in recent discussions of narrative: "what is it that propels narrative forward?" (1985, xix) The Move Grammar emphasizes the logical connections of the events of plot. It abstracts the surface features of the plot into a series of Problem/Solution couplets; the completion of a Solution constitutes a Move, which then causes subsequent events to occur. This, for Pavel, is a grammar that accounts for the generation of stories. He explicitly compares the Problem/Solution structure of the Move to the deep syntactic structures of generative grammar (1985, 15). It is, therefore, a syntax of plot not connected to the surface order of chronology or the order of presentation. Chronologically, for example, the Problem and its Solution may be separated by a long stretch of time filled with intervening events. The Move Grammar has been designed to account for the primary linkage of even widely separated Problems and Solutions and to relate subordinate events to this central structure as either leading to or leading away from this Solution. Similarly, the presentational order of events may diverge widely from the chronological order, as in the case of flashbacks, and from the Move structure, where the Solution may be presented before the Problem is known. The Move structure goes beyond both chronological order and presentational order to a more abstract level of syntactic organization, based on the strategic configurations of the plot.

Although the Move Grammar derives from earlier models of plot, such as those offered by Greimas, Todorov, Bremond, Prince, Dolezel, Van Dijk, and Ryan, Pavel stresses that it provides an improvement in three areas over previous models: "the implicitness of plot advance, the role of characters and groups of characters, and the links between plot and its meanings" (1985, 13). In many recent narrative grammars, plot is treated as an achronological symbolic system, a mere excipient of a set of contradictions embedded in the text. Most contemporary approaches to narrative are thus profoundly at odds with the intuitive understanding of plot as a linked sequence of actions. Pavel's system, on the other hand, is an "explicit formulation of the step-by-step unfolding of the plot" (1985, 14). It stresses the "logical and causal succession of actions" (1985, 34). It thus lends itself to the treatment of a historical narrative in a way that achronic systems, such as Lévi-Strauss's and Jameson's, do not, for it corresponds to our intuitive sense of historical representation in narrative form as fundamentally tied to the reciprocal links and advances of plot.

It also represents an advance over such stubbornly linear and sequential models of plot as that of Propp's *Morphology of the Folktale*. Whereas Propp's system could only deal with events in the sequential order of their occurrence, assigning meaning to the event only according to its position in the narrative, Pavel's system is able to find the interactive link between sequentially distant events: "A linear sequence narrative grammar produces strings of events whose unique, theoretically significant property is that they fill a certain position in the string . . . Propp's . . . 'functions' . . . combine among themselves in only one possible way. Consequently, every Proppian function can be defined by and only by its position in the sequence . . . What the Move-structure grammar adds to this is the idea that dependencies at a distance between narrative elements are themselves hierarchically organized" (1985, 17).

2. The study of narrative could be said to originate with the study of plot syntax. Approaches to the structure of plot have been considerably refined, however, from the original focus on plot functions associated with Vladimir Propp. Initially specified and defined by Propp in his breakthrough study of Russian folktales, the term "function" refers to the fundamental events or actions of the plot. Strung together, the functions comprise the basic structural level of narrative form. In Propp's analysis, the Russian folktale was shown to consist of thirty-one indispensable functions, such as Villainy, the Pursuit of the Hero, the Branding of the Hero, etc. Propp defined the function as "an act of a character, defined from the point of view of its significance for the course of the action" (1968, 21). Every folktale studied by Propp recapitulates a fixed structural pattern, both repeating these emblematic thirty-one functions and conforming to the precise consecutive order proposed in this model. While Propp's insistence on the exact and detailed adherence of each individual folk-narrative to this structural blueprint has been widely criticized and for the most part rejected by more recent theorists, the strength and impact of his original formulation remains. In isolating a set of narrative units called functions—which form a kind of universal bedrock of all narrative artifacts—Propp discovered a system and a structure that relate diverse narratives to one another as genetic variants of a single model. Where previously there had been only a numberless diversity of narratives, with no discernible structural features in common, the system developed in *The Morphology of the Folktale* disclosed a skeletal substructure that seemed to inform the vast majority of narrative plots. This concentration of plot functions as the framework of narrative form recalls as well Aristotle's privileging of actions in the *Poetics*, in which he states that actions, rather than characters, are the essential property of the story form.

3. The work of Claude Bremond attempts to specify precisely the system that regulates the pattern of narrative events, to comprehend the system of relays that leads from one narrative event to another. Bremond begins with the observation that many of the functions in a folktale are logical counterparts of one another and have a strong cause and effect relationship that is masked in the unilinear Proppian system by intervening functions. The Branding of the Hero, for example, (Propp's Function No. 17), structurally relates to the Recognition of the Hero (No. 27), yet the inherent logic underlying their adhesion is masked by the "indirection" of the plot. Bremond's project is to restore these logical relations: each function then is understood as an implied triadic sequence. 1. Situation opening a possiblity; 2. Actualization/nonactualization of possibility; 3. Success/Failure. Thus, a function must be understood as involving a potential *sequence* of occurrences, either actualized or latent. Accordingly, the basic unit of narrative discourse is understood in Bremond as the sequence, rather than the function, and the core structure of the sequence is seen as fundamentally triadic.

4. See Rick Altman (1984) for a treatment of genre in terms of syntactic and semantic forms of analysis.

5. Another way of looking at this sequence is to view it from the perspective of Greimas's spheres of activity (see Note 6). Greimas characterizes narrative exchanges in terms of three types: Communication, Desire, and Ordeal. The paradigm of Communication involves a Sender and a Receiver. The paradigm of Desire involves the actantial roles of Subject and Object, and the paradigm of Ordeal involves an Auxiliary and an Opponent. We can distinguish the two scenes involving Olmo and Alfredo in this fashion. Olmo participates here in the paradigm of Communication: he learns the code of the peasantry from the patriarch of the clan, and he recites this code. Moreover, the actantial roles that correspond to Communication are clearly embodied here. The patriarch transmits the code as a way of preparing Olmo for his journey out into the world. He functions as Greimas's Sender, charging Olmo with a kind of "mission" and indicating to Olmo the course of his future. Olmo plainly represents the Receiver, the recipient of knowledge and advice.

The exchange involving Alfredo at the dinner table corresponds, on the other hand, to Ordeal. His experience is one of pitched conflict with his father, mitigated somewhat by his alliance with his grandfather. Here the actantial roles correspond to the Opponent and the Helper, or Auxiliary. The Opponent is embodied in Alfredo's father, a figure who is portrayed as hostile to Alfredo throughout the film. Conflict seems to characterize all the relations between fathers and sons in the Berlinghieri household; the grandfather, in the role of Auxiliary, teams up with the young Alfredo, and together they stand in opposition to Giovanni, the father. Thus, by employing Greimas's model, we can see the way these parallel sequences actually involve very different types of narrative exchanges.

6. Since signification begins with binary oppositions in the structuralist view, the functions can only acquire semantic meaning through relations of opposition. Thus, for Greimas, Propp's system acquires its meaning through relations of opposition. Propp's thirty-one functions can therefore be rewritten as more general organizational patterns, featuring definite oppositional schemas: disjunction/conjunction, separation/ unification, struggle/reconciliation. Without attempting a universal narrative syntax, à la Propp, Greimas does isolate three distinct narrative syntagmas, that seem to recur throughout all narratives and that feature a binary structure: 1. performative syntagmas (tests, struggles); 2. contractual (establishing and breaking of contracts); 3. disjunctional (departures and returns). These three "major movements" are actually paradigmatic oppositions that in Greimas, as in Lévi-Strauss and Jakobson, are strung out sequentially along the distributional axis (Barthes 1977, 100). Each of these syntagmas implies a specific "actant" to perform the appropriate role; in Greimas, the actantial pairs correspond closely to the base syntagmas itemized above: Sender/Receiver (disjuntional syntagmas: the sphere of activity involving Communication); Subject/Object (contractual syntagmas: the sphere involving Desire); Auxiliary/Opponent (performative syntagmas: the sphere involving Ordeal).

7. This attempt to recode the essential structuration of narrative form in terms of highly abstract, highly analytic systems is characteristic of narratology after Propp.

In contemporary approaches, the concrete action of the plot, the empirical order of events — which is much in evidence in such Proppian functions as No. 23: "The hero, unrecognized, arrives home or in another country" — is stripped away to expose a deeper structural armature. This deep structure reveals itself, however, only when the plot is reencoded in other systems of analysis, such as linguistics, grammar, or modal logic. All of these separate approaches are championed by various theorists. The resulting schematic tables seem to have little to do with the indivisible and fixed order of sequences insisted upon by Propp, insofar as they largely ignore the crucial syntactic and syntagmatic axis in favor of an expanded paradigmatic analysis. In Lévi-Strauss, for example, the analysis of myth proceeds by initially breaking up the lateral syntagmatic relations; the argument for this methodological criterion is strengthened by the fact that the "plot structure" in mythic texts is already quite disjointed. By setting the functions in paradigmatic groups, the logic of the myth emerges at a deeper antinomic level — it reveals its binary core — which is concealed by the motivated connectedness and pseudo-casuality of the plot. This privileging of the paradigmatic alternatives called forth by the individual functions has been adopted as the dominant view in Saussurean-influenced narratology. A new definition of plot functions has thus emerged: the lateral movement of the plot, the syntagmatic unfolding of the "chain of events" was understood to be a *projection* of the set of paradigmatic oppositions onto the syntagmatic, distributional axis. As Barthes writes: "all contemporary researchers begin with Lévi-Strauss' proposition that 'the order of chronological succession is reabsorbed into an atemporal matrix structure'" (1977, 98). Vladimir Propp, for his part, disputes this revision of the functional level of the text: in a little-known reply to Lévi-Strauss, Propp argues that the founder of structural anthropology is not involved in narrative analysis at all, that narrative, by definition, is the causally motivated stitching together of events (1984, 67–81).

Chapter Three: Analysis of the Character-System of *1900*

1. The breakthrough in plot analysis associated with the work of Vladimir Propp brought with it a significant revision of the conceptualization of the literary character. Traditionally, the character had been seen as a facsimile of the person, a replica, that is, of the human being, endowed with personal singularity and psychological coherence and armed with a motivation that carried the plot. The analysis of traditional folkloric narratives, however, such as Propp's study of Russian folktales, opened up a new perspective on the question of character. The hero of a fairy tale, being without psychological depth or biographical density, functions not as a complex and nuanced personality, but rather as the simple performer of essential narrative actions whose purpose it is to advance and facilitate the movement of the plot.

Propp designates these narrative operators "Agents" and provides an itemized set of *dramatis personae* such as the Villain, the Donor, and the Princess. Since Propp, this concept has been applied to a range of narrative and dramatic forms, with interesting and original results. The most striking transformation brought about by this shift is that the character, seen simply as the performer of narrative actions, is endowed not with an old-fashioned repertory of personal attributes, but with a purely virtual significance. The significance of the character is entirely dependent upon how he or she is "predicated." The notion of character as a human facsimile, who arrived in the narrative fully individuated with a personal history and an inventory of attributes, surrenders its central importance at the basic structural level of narrative form. The Agent of narrative must be understood, in Todorov's words, "as a blank form which is completed by different predicates" (Todorov 1977, 110).

This functional definition of the character as the Agent of narrative events acquired a new importance in the structuralist disciplines that emerged around the work of Claude Lévi-Strauss and Roman Jakobson in the 1960s. At this time the study of narrative was given a decisive linguistic orientation. Given the likelihood that a similar formal organization orders all semantic systems, a homological relationship was posited between sentence and narrative discourse. In *Elements of Structural Syntax*, A. J. Greimas and L. Tesniere (1965) liken the structure of a sentence to that of narrative in that all the elements of snytax contribute to a certain end or resolution. Stressing the interchangeable nature of the diverse parts of speech in the context of the sentence as a whole, the authors characterize the "actant" as that part of speech that performs the essential function required for the sentence to be completed. The sentence can be predicative, like a "little drama," or circumstantial, as in a "little situation." These two conditions of drama and situation correspond, respectively, to the dynamic and the stative or descriptive sequences in a narrative. In each case, the different parts of speech can assume different functions in the sentence, much as diverse organs in biology can take on diverse vital functions. The grammatical part of speech is subordinate to the semantic function it performs, just as the actant of narrative is surrogated to the events of the plot, serving as a kind of deputy or delegate to the various "spheres of action" vital to the story.

As the structural operator of the underlying narrative transformations, the actant is linked to the narrative level of functions or spheres of action that constitute a kind of deep, indispensable structural armature of the narrative artifact. The distinction between the *deep structure* of the narrative and the *surface discourse* is crucial. The surface features include stylistic attributes, the reported discourse of the characters, and the authorial descriptions of setting and so forth, whereas the deep structure is comprised of an irreducible syntax of action and event, either actual or potential. The concept of the actant pertains to the deep structural level of the narrative and not to the surface properties of the discourse. According to Tomashevsky, the category of the character is not even an intrinsic part of narrative structure: "The protagonist is by no means an essential part of the story. The story, as a system of motifs, may dispense entirely with him and his characteristics. The protagonist, rather, is the result of the formation of the story material into a plot. On the one hand he is a means of stringing motifs together; and on the other, he embodies the motivation which connects the motifs" (Tomashevsky 1965, 90). (In Tomashevsky's usage, "motifs" correspond to Propp's "functions" and are characterized as static or dynamic.) The literary phenomenon of the single, individuated character, then, can be "analytically dissolved" through a process of "actantial reduction" to show that this character actually condenses the operation of two very different actants (Jameson 1981, 126).

A. J. Greimas borrowed the term actant from Tesniere in his synthetic reworking of the Proppian Agents and the "dramatic functions" of Etienne Souriau, who had given an early structuralist account of the actantial system of dramatic literature. The Greimas synthesis marks a clear conceptual advance over the previous "inventories," which tended to be somewhat random in their enumeration of different roles. Greimas stresses the *logical relations* between the actants. He distills from Propp's seven *dramatis personae* and Souriau's six dramatic functions three logical pairs of actantial com-

binations that recur throughout all narratives in a kind of genetic pattern: Sender/
Receiver; Subject-Hero/Object-Value; and Auxiliary/Opponent. These rudimentary oppositions are embodied in characters that are circulated in the text like playing cards.
Brought into conflictual relationships, their opposition develops temporally into the
story.

In Greimas's system, the actantial categories combine into pairs quite naturally: the
Subject category calls forth the Object category; the operation of a Sender presupposes
the existence of a Receiver; an Auxiliary assumes the activity of an Opponent. These
paired actants participate accordingly in three main spheres of activity or semantic
axes: Desire, Communication, and Ordeal. The emphasis on binary oppositions, deriving from structural linguistics, is carried over into Greimas's conception of plot patterns, which are seen to be organized around the basic pairs of disjunction/conjunction
and separation/unification.

2. Jameson devises a narrative method based on the "semiotic rectangle" of Greimas,
which allows him to "transcode," or simultaneously correlate, ideology and narrative
structure, ideology and the primary narratological levels of function and actant. In
many ways, this is a major theoretical accomplishment. In *The Prison House of Language* (1972), Jameson sketches in the preliminary version of this model. Here the text's
projection of ideological closure is linked directly to the deep-structural level of story
events (Jameson 1972, 164). Even more, the drive toward ideological and conceptual closure *produces* the plot events out of the symbolic matrix already energized by the text—
a perfect reversal of the basic order of fabula and sjuzhet.

The method draws from the text a set of paradigmatic oppostitions and threads
them onto Greimas's semiotic rectangle. Greimas's system provides several advantages,
for rather than imposing a system of static binary oppositions on the text, it maps
the object into a four-part arrangement, consisting of the principal oppositional pair
and two corresponding minor oppositions, or "simple negations," which also both oppose and complement the major pair (1972, 164). The key elements of the text are ar-
ranged in units of major and minor oppositions. Generating a continuous displacement
from one term to another, the system *produces story events* out of the movement between the four terms, a movement driven by the antinomy that haunts the work. "[In]
this sense to "articulate" the mechanism would mean repeatedly to try out one term
after another, in order to measure the gap between them. Such articulation would thus
be perfectly consistent with the narrative form as such, where the mind is confronted
with a series of imaginative possibilities in succession" (1972, 164).

In *The Political Unconscious*, Jameson shifts the use of the semiotic rectangle to the
actantial level of the narrative, applying it to the character-system, whose members
are systematized into positions of complementarity or opposition. Applied to both the
functional and the actantial levels, the semiotic rectangle serves to account for all the
symbolic positions available to the text, thus indicating its particular form of ideological closure, specifying the terms beyond which the text cannot go. The text rotates
these terms in order to find a logical solution, a process Jameson describes as the
"prestidigitation of narrative," the resolution of real contradictions in symbolic form.
From the particular technique and the specific failures of this prestidigitation, history
can be read.

Chapter Six: Narrative "Voice: Parallel Editing and the Moving Camera

1. While we have seen one dimension in which this type of overview is established in the analysis of tense, the standard theoretical threatments of narrative form, such as Genette's, separate the categories of tense and voice. Accordingly, I will observe this partition in an effort to structure the overall analysis of *1900* along the established lines of narratological inquiry.

REFERENCES

Althusser, Louis. 1971. *Lenin and Philosophy*. London: New Left Books.
————. 1984. "Reply to John Lewis." In *Essays on Ideology*. London: Verso.
Altman, Rick. 1984. "A Semantic/Syntactic Approach to Film Genre." *Cinema Journal* 23.3 (Spring): 6–18.
Attali, Jacques. 1985. *Noise*. Translated by Brian Massumi. Minneapolis: University of Minnesota Press.
Bal, Mieke. 1983. "The Narrating and the Focalizing: A Theory of the Agents in Narrative." *Style* 17.2 (Spring): 234–68.
————. 1985. *Narratology: Introduction to the Theory of Narrative*. Translated by Christine von Boheemen. Toronto: University of Toronto Press.
Balibar, Etienne. 1977. *Theoretical Practice* 7/8. Quoted in Claire Johnston, *Edinburgh Magazine* 2: 5–7.
Barthes, Roland. 1977. *Image-Music-Text*. Translated by Stephen Heath. New York: Hill and Wang.
Bataille, Georges. 1971. *Literature and Evil*. New York: Urizen Books.
Bennett, Tony. 1979. *Formalism and Marxism*. London: Methuen.
Benveniste, Emile. 1971. *Problems in General Linguistics*. Translated by Mary Elizabeth Meek. Coral Gables: University of Miami Press.
Bertolucci, Bernardo. 1971. Interview with Amos Vogel. *Film Comment* (Fall).
————. 1975. "Films Are Animal Events." Interview with Gideon Bachmann. *Film Quarterly* 29.1 (Autumn): 11–19.
————. 1977. "History Lessons." Interview with Deborah Young. *Film Comment* (November): 16–19.
————. 1983. "The Poetry of Class Struggle." Interview with Fabio di Vico and Robert Degni. In *The Cineaste Interviews*, edited by Dan Georgakas and Lenny Rubenstein, 138–148. Chicago: Lake View Press.
Bordwell, David. 1985. *Narration in the Fiction Film*. Madison: University of Wisconsin Press.
Branigan, Edward. 1984. *Point of View in the Cinema*. New York: Mouton.
Bremond, Claude. 1973. *Logique du Recit*. Paris: Seuil.

References

Casetti, Franscesco. 1986. "Antonioni and Hitchcock: Two Strategies of Narrative Investment." *Sub-Stance* 51: 69–86.

Chatman, Seymour. 1986a. "Characters and Narrators: Filter, Center, Slant and Interest-focus." *Poetics Today* 7.2: 189–204.

———. 1986b. Review of *Point of View in the Cinema,* by Edward Branigan. *Film Quarterly* 40.1 (Fall): 45–46.

———. 1987. "Reply to Edward Branigan." *Film Quarterly* 41.1 (Fall): 63–65.

———. Forthcoming. *Coming to Terms.*

Dolezel, Lubomir. 1976. "Narrative Worlds." In *Sound, Sign and Meaning,* edited by L. Matejka, 542–53. Ann Arbor: University of Michigan Press.

———. 1983. "Intensional Function, Invisible Worlds, and Franz Kafka." *Style* 17.2 (Spring): 129–41.

Foucault, Michel. 1977. "Nietzsche, Genealogy, History." In *Language, Counter-Memory, Practice.* Ithaca: Cornell University Press.

Gaudreault, André. 1987. "Narration and Monstration in the Cinema." *Journal of Film and Video* 39 (Spring): 29–36.

———. 1988. *Du littéraire au filmique: système du recit.* Quebec: Les Presses de l'Université à Laval.

Genette, Gerard. 1977. *Narrative Discourse: An Essay in Method.* Translated by Jane E. Lewin. Ithaca: Cornell University Press.

Gramsci, Antonio. 1971. *Selections from the Prison Notebooks.* Edited and translated by Q. Hoare and G. Nowell-Smith. London: Lawrence and Wishart.

Greimas, Algirdas. 1987. *On Meaning.* Translated by Paul J. Perron and Frank H. Collins. Minneapolis: University of Minnesota Press.

Greimas, Algirdas and Lucien Tesniere. 1965. *Elements of Structural Syntax.* Paris: Klincksieck.

———. 1973. "Les actants, les acteurs, et les figures." In *Semiotique narrative et textuelle.* Edited by Claude Chabrol. Paris: Larousse.

Gunning, Tom. Forthcoming. *D. W. Griffith and the Origins of American Narrative Film.* Champaign: University of Illinois Press.

Henderson, Brian. 1983. "Tense, Mood and Voice in Film." *Film Quarterly* (Fall): 4–17.

Hindess, Barry, and Paul Hirst. 1975. *Precapitalist Modes of Production.* London: Routledge and Kegan Paul.

Horton, Andrew. 1980. "History as Myth and Myth as History in Bertolucci's *1900.*" *Film and History* 10.1: 9–15.

Jameson, Fredric. 1972. *The Prison-House of Language.* Princeton: Princeton University Press.

———. 1981. *The Political Unconscious.* Ithaca: Cornell University Press.

———. 1982. Interview with Leonard Green, Jonathan Culler, and Richard Klein. *Diacritics* 12.3 (Fall): 72–91.

———. 1988. "Marxism and Historicism." In *The Ideologies of Theory.* Vol. 2, 148–177.

Johnston, Claire. 1977. "Introduction." *Edinburgh Magazine* 2: 5–7.

Kolker, Robert Phillip. 1985. *Bernardo Bertolucci.* New York: Oxford University Press.

Kristeva, Julia. 1981. "Women's Time." Translated by Alice Jardine and Harry Blake. *Signs: Journal of Women in Culture and Society* 7.1 (Autumn): 13–35.

Lévi-Strauss, Claude. 1963. *Structural Anthropology.* New York: Basic Books.

Marx, Karl. *Economic and Philosophical Manuscripts,* Second Manuscript, "Private Property and Communism," Section 4. In *Early Writings,* translated by Rodney Livingstone and Gregor Benton. London: Penguin/NLB, 1975.

Mohanty, S. P. 1982. "History at the Edge of Discourse: Marxism, Culture, Interpretation." *Diacritics* 12.3 (Fall): 33–46.

Mulvey, Laura. 1989. "Changes: Thoughts on Myth, Narrative and Historical Experience." In *Visual and Other Pleasures*. Indiana University Press.

Nowell-Smith, Geoffrey. 1968. *Visconti*. Cinema World Series. New York: Doubleday.

———. 1977. "On the Writing of the History of the Cinema: Some Problems." *Edinburgh Magazine* 2: 8–12.

Pavel, Thomas. 1979. *Move-Grammar: An Exploration of Literary Semantics*. Toronto Linguistic Circle, Prepublication.

———. 1980. "Narrative Domains." *Poetics Today* 1.4 (Summer): 105–14.

———. 1981. "Borders of Fiction." Paper presented at the MLA Conference, New York, December.

———. 1985. *The Poetics of Plot*. Minneapolis: University of Minnesota Press.

Propp, Vladimir. 1968. *The Morphology of the Folktale*. Translated by Laurence Scott. Austin: University of Texas Press.

———. 1976. "Study of the Folktale: Structure and History." *Dispositio* 3 (Autumn): 277–92.

———. 1984. *Theory and History of Folklore*. Edited by Anatoly Liberman, translated by Ariadna Y. Martin and Richard P. Martin. Minneapolis: University of Minnesota Press.

Ricoeur, Paul. 1980. "Narrative Time." *Critical Inquiry* 7.1: 169–90.

———. 1984. *Time and Narrative*. Vol. 1. Chicago: University of Chicago Press.

Rimmon-Kenan, Shlomith. 1983. *Narrative Fiction: Contemporary Poetics*. London: Methuen.

Rosen, Philip. 1984. "Securing the Historical." In *Cinema Histories, Cinema Practices*, edited by Patricia Mellencamp and Philip Rosen. Frederick, Md.: University Publications of America.

Ryan, Marie-Laure. 1981. "The Pragmatics of Personal and Impersonal Narration." *Poetics* 10: 517–39.

Sorlin, Pierre. 1980. *The Film in History*. New York: Barnes and Noble.

Todorov, Tzvetan. 1977. *The Poetics of Prose*. Translated by Richard Howard. Ithaca: Cornell University Press.

Tomashevsky, Boris. 1965. "Thematics." In *Russian Formalist Criticism*, edited by Lee T. Lemon and Marion J. Reis. Lincoln: University of Nebraska Press.

White, Hayden. 1973. *Metahistory*. Baltimore: Johns Hopkins University Press.

———. 1978. Tropics of Discourse. Baltimore: Johns Hopkins University Press.

———. 1980. "The Value of Narrativity in the Representation of Reality." *Critical Inquiry* 7.1: 5–27.

———. 1982. "Getting Out of History." *Diacritics* 12.3 (Fall): 2–13.

———. 1987. "Getting Out of History: Jameson's Redemption of Narrative." In *The Content of the Form*. Baltimore: Johns Hopkins University Press.

Williams, Brooke. 1985. *History and Semiotic*. Toronto: Victory University, Toronto Semiotic Circle.

Wilson, George. 1986. *Narration in Light: Studies in Cinematic Point of View*. Baltimore: Johns Hopkins University Press.

Zemon-Davis, Natalie. 1988. "Film and the Challenge of Authenticity." *The Yale Review*: 457–82.

INDEX

175

Index